D1565931

Strategy and Finance
in
Higher Education

Strategy and Finance
in
Higher Education

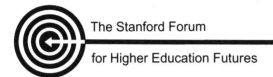

The Stanford Forum

for Higher Education Futures

William F. Massy and Joel W. Meyerson
Editors

Peterson's Guides
Princeton, New Jersey

Library of Congress Cataloging-in-Publication Data

    Strategy and finance in higher education / William F. Massy and Joel W. Meyerson, editors.
        p. cm.
    Includes bibliographical references.
    ISBN 1-56079-178-0
    1. Universities and colleges—United States—Administration—
Congresses. 2. Education, Higher—United States—Finance—Congresses.
I. Massy, William F., 1943–   II. Meyerson, Joel W., 1951– .
LB2341.S837   1992
378.73—dc20   92-12863

Composition and design by Peterson's Guides

Printed in the United States of America

10 9 8 7 6 5 4 3 2 1

Contents ————————————

Contributors

Editors

William F. Massy is the director of the Stanford Institute for Higher Education Research and is professor of education and business administration at the university. Massy was the university's chief financial officer from 1990 to 1991, vice president for finance from 1989 to 1990, vice president for business and finance from 1977 to 1989, vice provost for research from 1971 to 1977, and associate dean of the Stanford Graduate School of Business in 1971. He is author and coauthor of several books, including *Endowment: Principles, Policies, and Management, Planning Models for Colleges and Universities,* and *Stochastic Models of Buying Behavior,* and numerous journal articles.

Joel W. Meyerson is codirector with William Massy of the Stanford Forum for Higher Education Futures and is a partner and director of the higher education and nonprofit practices of Coopers & Lybrand. Previously, he codirected the Forum for College Financing at Columbia University. He has served on several advisory panels, including the Massachusetts Board of Regents task forces on capital maintenance and tuition policy, and has taught at the Harvard Institute for Educational Management. Meyerson has authored or coauthored many publications, including *Productivity and Higher Education, Strategic Analysis: Using Comparative Data to Better Understand Your Institution,* and *Higher Education in a Changing Economy.*

Essayists

Richard Chait serves as director of the Center for Higher Education Governance and Leadership and is professor of higher education and management at the University of Maryland in College Park. Previously he was Mandel Professor of Nonprofit Management at Case Western Reserve University and associate provost of Penn State University. From 1974 to 1979 he was director and later educational chairman of the Institute for Educational Management (IEM) at Harvard University, where he was an assistant professor in the Graduate School of Education. His recent publications have focused on college and university boards of trustees and application of management techniques to academic organizations.

Michael Finnerty has been at Yale since Spetember 1984. As vice president for finance and administration, he is responsible for financial and non-academic administrative affairs. Previously, since 1973, he had been associated with the executive and legislative branches of the New York State government as director of the budget and as the chief financial and economic adviser to Governor Mario M. Cuomo. Before being named director, Finnerty was chief of staff to Governor Hugh L. Carey.

Nannerl O. Keohane has been president of Wellesley College since 1981, where she also serves as a professor of political science. Before accepting the post at Wellesley, Keohane was a faculty member at Stanford University, Swarthmore College, and the University of Pennsylvania. Keohane is a coeditor of *Feminist Theory: A Critique of Ideology* and author of *Philosophy and the State in France: The Renaissance to the Enlightenment.*

Susan M. Schaffer is the vice president for administrative resources at Stanford University. She also serves on the university's operation council and has been on the steering committee for the university's budget repositioning effort. Prior to joining Stanford in 1989, she worked for United Airlines for nineteen years, serving the last ten as a vice president and corporate officer.

Ann L. Sowder is a senior vice president of Standard & Poor's Ratings Group, located in their Western Regional Office in San Francisco. She has business development responsibilities for S&P's tax-exempt and taxable-debt rating services, as well as analytical responsibilities in the tax-exempt revenue bond areas of higher education, transportation, and special taxes. Sowder has been involved with the ratings of numerous public and private higher education institutions nationwide. Her involvement has been in the roles of both rating agency analyst and investment banker, having spent seven years in the public finance division of a major New York–based investment banking firm.

Timothy R. Warner is associate vice president and director of university budgets at Stanford University. He is responsible under the provost for directing the development of Stanford's operating and capital budgets. In this capacity, over the past two years, he has been closely involved in a strategic planning effort that has reduced Stanford's budget and brought about downsizing across the university. He is a fellow at the Stanford Institute for Higher Education Research, a member of the Pew Higher Education Research Program, and a Stanford representative to the Consortium on Financing Higher Education.

Gilbert R. Whitaker Jr. became provost and vice president for academic affairs at the University of Michigan in September 1990 after serving as dean and professor of business economics in the School of Business Administration for nearly twelve years. His academic specialty is managerial economics. Previously, Whitaker was dean and professor of business economics at the M. J. Neeley School of Business at Texas Christian University and associate dean and professor of business economics at the Graduate School of Business at Washington University in St. Louis. He is coauthor of *Business Economics: Principles and Cases*.

Preface ─────────────────────────────

The Stanford Forum for Higher Education Futures is a national research center resident at Stanford University. Its mission is to improve the strategy, finance, and management of American colleges and universities. The Stanford Forum helps college and university officers and governing boards respond to new imperatives, develop viable institutional strategies, and implement them through effective finance and management. It conducts and sponsors research and disseminates knowledge through symposia, retreats, books, and monographs. Forum fellows include leaders and innovators in higher education and industry. The Stanford Forum is the successor to the Forum for College Financing, which was resident at Columbia University.

Introduction

William F. Massy
Joel W. Meyerson

Any enterprise as magnificent and original as American higher education will continuously undergo change. Change is the genius of greatness. Sometimes change will be highly visible, other times barely perceptible. Sometimes change will be turbulent, leaping forward after a period of silence; at other times it will be slow, making steady, incremental progress. Change is the process of renewal, of refreshment, of growth. Change is the process of hope.

American higher education has entered into a period of visible, turbulent change. Spurred by outside forces, colleges and universities are transforming themselves, challenging cherished assumptions, testing new paradigms. The "disturbance in the field" that is sweeping higher education has been triggered by many factors, most notably several external forces converging at once. They include eroding public support, shifting demographic patterns, an anemic national economy, the ongoing American "retreat" from government at all levels, the inability of families to afford tuition, and successive revenue shortfalls and budget deficits at many institutions that have weakened their financial and physical infrastructures. As a result, many institutions have turned inward, entering an era of "active introspection." Many are engaged, for the first time, in deliberate, systematic planning. Recognizing that they no longer can be all things to all people, they are seeking to define their mission, identify priorities, and be financially realistic.

Strategy and higher education do not represent a natural match. In fact, past experience produces ample evidence that institutions spurn planning like a body rejecting a new organ. Some in higher education share an unassailable faith with adherents of pure capitalism—namely, the system works best on its own, with no tampering or tuning, with an "invisible hand" providing all the guidance necessary.

All this is changing. What's different now are the *necessity of change,* driven by relentless outside forces laying siege to all sides of the academy, and the *possibility of success* as more and more institutions successfully plan for and manage change. This is what this book, *Strategy and Finance in Higher Education,* is about. It starts with a discussion of the strategy process, explaining the perspective of three key players—the board, the president, and the senior financial staff. Next it takes an in-depth look at the planning process at two major institutions, Stanford University and the University of Michigan. Finally, it examines a somewhat unorthodox way of assessing how well institutional planning and change are working.

Several common themes emerge in the following papers: Planning and change create significant stress on campus; the considerable confusion of planning participants' roles and responsibilities requires careful sorting; planning is a consensual, collaborative experience, with the key participants working closely together; planning should generally involve a broad cross-section of the institutional community; planning often requires cultural change on campus to be successful; planning and plans benefit greatly from flexibility.

Three other themes, touched lightly in this book, warrant special mention because, in some respects, they represent paradigm shifts that promise to make change possible. The first pertains to *quality.* It wasn't too long ago that it was *verboten* to discuss cost on campus, and quality was synonymous with expenditures—the more money that could be spent on a project, the higher its purported value. Now American industry—and higher education—have discovered that this is not always the case. Organizations *can* produce higher quality products and services at lower costs, and "low-cost providers" enjoy comparative advantages that make them more successful organizations. For higher education this means that institutions that reduce costs will have more resources to invest in future quality enhancements. The second theme is *accountability.* As they seek to respond to widespread public skepticism, institutions are becoming less insular and more accountable than previously. Institutions are trying to defuse the public perception that they are self-serving and place their interests above national goals. They also are becoming more attentive to the public concerns about academic performance as the relative competitiveness of our work force continues to decline. The third theme is *technology.* There is increasing evidence that the long-heralded technological revolution in higher education is close at hand. Technologies are being tested that will dramatically improve academic productivity—and quality. It is safe to say that as the American classroom is "reengineered," the American college will be "reinvented."

THE STRATEGY PROCESS

The Trustees' Role

Although boards of trustees play an intrinsic and irreplaceable role in the strategy process, confusion often surrounds their participation. This confusion, according to Richard Chait of the Center for Higher Education Governance and Leadership at the University of Maryland, can be traced to two sources: the *character* of most boards, namely, lay bodies that meet intermittently, and the *demands* of shaping strategy for a very complex organization in a highly competitive environment.

The board's role in planning can be clarified by dividing the strategy process into four distinct phases and assessing the role of the board in each phase.

The first phase is *envisioning.* Chait describes the board as the "organization's DNA," storing a historical blueprint of the institution. Boards are singularly equipped to make a pivotal contribution in the envisioning stage. Trustees have a keen sense of the institution's past, a large (but not too detailed) picture of its present, and a long-term focus on the institution's future.

Formulating strategy is the second phase. It is the process by which an institution wrestles a vision of the future into the realm of reality. It is in this phase, according to Chait, that the board makes its greatest contribution—not by doing the work but by ensuring that the work gets done. The board should be essentially *reactive* with respect to strategy formation, leading largely with questions, not answers.

Implementing strategy is the third phase. Here, with few exceptions, the board is not a key player. Rather, during implementation the board should lead by example and keep the institution focused on its strategic plan. The board's agenda should be explicitly linked to the institution's overall strategic priorities.

The fourth phase is *monitoring strategy.* Chait believes that there may be no more critical role for the board than to compel measurement of performance—the effects and pace of progress toward enactment of an institution's vision. In this way the board enables the institution it governs to realize its ambitions.

In today's environment the board must also play a role in reducing costs and *resizing* an institution. Chait believes that the board must be the strongest voice on campus for fiscal prudence. And when constraints are criticized, it must be unequivocally steadfast or risk jeopardizing the presidency as well as the strategy.

The President's Role

Presidents, too, make substantial contributions to institutional planning. However, like that of trustees, their role may be shrouded in mystery. Nannerl O. Keohane, President of Wellesley College, identifies three hurdles presidents must overcome to be effective planners.

The first hurdle springs from the assumption that presidents have little sense of *continuity* with their past and are primarily motivated by a desire to leave a mark on their institutions. Keohane argues that thinking broadly about the course of an institution—its past, present, and future—is the single most important part of the president's job. Presidents, at the focal point of many forces within and outside the institution, have a unique vantage point that promotes broad, strategic thinking. Successful presidents, Keohane suggests, have a humbling sense of themselves as part of a long line of leadership and are able to transcend their own time in office and think creatively about the future.

The second hurdle stems from the belief held by some presidents that planning for the future is of little value and therefore they should expend their efforts elsewhere. Keohane maintains that properly done, strategic planning is quite valuable. While it is easy to get off track—perhaps by getting lost in data or trying to predict the future with too much precision—it is unwise to dismiss the utility of strategic planning simply because it *might* fail.

The third hurdle is rooted in the conventional wisdom that advises presidents to focus on the planning *process* rather than products, since products rarely resemble the future as it actually unfolds. While Keohane believes that process *is* important, she believes that the product—a sense of destination and a path for getting there—is critical. The president's involvement at this stage is crucial, since he or she must focus participants' energies on the final product and avoid becoming mired in the planning process.

The infusion of vision with a sustained sense of desired outcomes, Keohane believes, is the essence of presidential leadership. In addition to helping to maintain focus, the president can make several other contributions to the planning process: defining the scope of the planning enterprise, assembling and charging appropriate participants, effectively communicating the plan to all parts of the institution at every stage, and finally, sustaining the symbiosis between ideas and implementation so that planning does not end abruptly when a report is issued.

The Chief Financial Officer's Role

Along with the board and the president, the chief financial officer (CFO) is a key partner in the planning leadership of an institution. Although more in synch with the need for planning and control than many other members of the academy, the CFO may be viewed with suspicion in this area. According to Michael Finnerty, vice president for finance at Yale University, this is attributable, in part, to the tension between *centralized* financial operations and *decentralized* academic programs. Often the financial function is viewed as a barrier to increasing the quality and size of academic programs. Rather, Finnerty argues, in a time of economic constraint, the financial office must be seen as a protector and supporter of academic quality. That is, the role of the CFO should be, whenever possible, to responsibly finance the maximum direct program activity possible.

At Yale the planning process started with an assessment of investment needs for facilities. Once the scope of the problem became clear, faculty, development, and other administrative officers—in addition to the CFO—became extensively involved in the effort. The goal was to address critical facilities needs without undermining academic programs. To this end, academic program needs were also assessed.

The financial office analyzed academic and facilities requirements within the framework of realistic resource constraints. It then presented planning alternatives to the university community.

To succeed, Finnerty believes, planning must encompass all aspects of institutional life and broadly involve the university community. Ultimately the CFO must be perceived as an ally of the academic leadership.

APPROACHES TO PLANNING

The Michigan Experience

An anomaly of sorts is occurring at the University of Michigan. While a formal planning process may not actually exist, many of the fruits of successful planning—reduced operating costs, increased academic quality—are currently being harvested. Gilbert Whitaker, provost at the University of Michigan, traces these changes to a collective understanding that the *cul-*

ture of the university needed to change. The need for culture change was spelled out in a report entitled "Enhancing Quality in an Era of Resource Constraints." Prepared under the auspices of the provost, the report called for innovation by substitution (in lieu of incremental growth) and decision making driven by customer, cost, and quality considerations. The report led to several cost-cutting changes in administrative activities as well as cuts in services, changes in faculty workloads, and new revenue-generating programs. The following activities, known as "Excellence on a Revenue Diet," were also undertaken.

PACE task force. This task force—Provost's Advisory Committee on Excellence—focused on academic units, attempting to allocate both costs and revenues. Known as "conscious net support" (CNS), this approach computes the net financial support received by a unit so that it can be reviewed in a priority context during the budgeting process.

Enrollment management. Following up on the PACE reports, deans have been assigned to review historical data on applications, admissions, and yield in an effort to predict and manage enrollment and, likewise, revenues.

Annual budget actions. As a result of a reduction in its state appropriation, the university had to significantly roll back its expenses. Whitaker describes how those cuts were made based on enrollment data, the relative subsidies indicated by the PACE CNS model, and perceptions of quality. The steps taken were actually not much different than those for previous cuts; they were, however, crucial steps toward aligning annual budgets with longer-term plans.

Space costs. Michigan is beginning an effort to charge units for space, previously a free good. They expect to produce more accurate accounting of unit costs and more efficient use of space.

Total quality management. Whitaker believes that a change in style to total quality management is essential to Michigan's future. The institution began the process with an executive retreat during which draft mission and vision statements were developed. The statements are filled with good ideas embracing the spirit and values of the university and will serve as a guide to the university in the coming years.

The Stanford Experience

Strategic change at Stanford University started on the administrative side of the campus. It involved changing the administrative culture as well as improving organization, budgeting, and decision making.

A budget crisis, low growth, and poor staff morale associated with a tarnished image have wrought extraordinary change at Stanford. Susan Schaffer, former vice president for administration, describes how Stanford set out to create a separate administrative culture—quite distinct from the faculty culture—by adapting aspects of the corporate model to the university's needs. She dubs the new administrative culture the "topline," which focuses the administration's efforts on what ought to be its *raison d'être:* support of the school's academic and research missions. Schaffer identifies six building blocks to make the topline concept a reality.

A strategic plan. The plan includes a specific mission statement, a set of goals to achieve the mission, and strategies and tactics to achieve those goals. Further, the plan provides context and focus for the administration's action and helps to explain and justify these actions to the faculty, with the aim of improving relations.

Organizational focus and clarity. Each administrative unit conducted a thorough self-study to determine its own mission and value, as well as its products, services, and consumers. This focus "leans up" the administration by ensuring that each unit has a tight fit with the purpose of the institution.

Measurement systems. Measurement entails laying out benchmark performance indicators critical to achieving a results orientation. Schaffer describes great resistance to measurement at Stanford, as it raised issues of autonomy and control. According to her, however, autonomy is a faculty domain, not an administrative one.

Individual objectives and evaluation systems. Evaluating performance calls for personal evaluations based not just on relationships with superiors or management skills but also on measurable results. Individuals are held accountable for achieving a set of clearcut objectives.

Communication channels. Schaffer recommends the creation of formal and frequent opportunities for staff to understand and discuss the mission, focus, and issues that face their unit, the administration, and the university. This aspect of the new culture also represented a significant change from the generally autonomous nature of the university.

Defining an administrative culture. Critical leadership is essential to provide administrative clarity, definition, and groundedness. It provides a platform from which the administration can act with confidence.

Schaffer believes that the new culture will bring an elevated sense of self and pride to the administrative staff. Most important, the topline orientation will provide the stabilization needed for Stanford's financial future.

Maintaining academic excellence at Stanford also involved overhauling the budgeting process. The 1980s were a period of extraordinary growth there, according to Tim Warner, Director of University Budgets. However, amid this boom, signs of a coming contraction began to appear—a planned budget deficit was approved by the board, indirect cost rates were driven upward by rising construction and infrastructure costs, decision making was becoming gridlocked, and tuition increases were being harshly criticized. (Of course, no one could have predicted the maelstrom that was about to descend on Stanford.)

In response to these emerging challenges, Stanford set out to reduce its budget and change its organization. Although these efforts fall into four distinct phases, Warner cautions that they do *not* encompass a planned, integrated approach. Rather, each phase was a response to a new crisis.

Phase One was called "Action Plan for Change" (APC). An APC "steering committee," made up of the provost, a dean, and several vice presidents, conducted over 100 interviews with faculty, staff, and administrators. From these discussions four operating principles emerged: simplify organizational structures, simplify processes, develop stronger customer relationships, and change the culture to make these principles work. However, before specific recommendations could be developed, the outside world—an earthquake and a sharp drop in the growth rate of government research—intervened.

Phase Two was called "Repositioning." Its aim was to provide balanced budgets in the future. To achieve this, *administrative* expenses would be reduced by 13 percent, or $22 million. Other objectives of repositioning were to hold tuition growth to inflation plus one percent, to expand APC efforts in process and structural reform, and to constrain building growth.

Phase Three entailed a *reorganization* of the central administration. The goals of this restructuring were to elevate the position of the deans, to strengthen the relationship between the schools and support services, and to clarify the responsibilities of the vice presidents. This reorganization defined policy roles, responsibility, and accountability more clearly, albeit at the cost of additional vice presidencies—which was viewed by some as contradictory to the university's repositioning goals.

Phase Four occurred at the height of Stanford's dispute with the federal government. As a result of the indirect cost controversy (and other factors),

Stanford had to reduce its operating budget by $43 million. Both academic and nonacademic budgets were subject to reduction, and some revenue sources were targeted for increase.

Will Stanford emerge as a different institution? Not fundamentally, according to Warner. He expresses the university's belief that the organizational change and budget reductions in process will allow Stanford to achieve its financial objectives without a basic redesign of the institution.

MONITORING CHANGE

How effective is strategic change in higher education? One approach is to monitor the reaction of the capital markets to institutional change—that is, is credit quality improving or declining? This is similar to how the share prices of corporations reflect investor assessment or performance.

Ann Sowder, senior vice president of Standard & Poors Ratings Group (which assigns ratings to college and university debt), believes that the overall creditworthiness of higher education is in a "stable" position. This, in effect, reflects a strong market endorsement of the change currently under way at many institutions. Sowder acknowledges that on the one hand, colleges and universities face a period of declining growth and retrenchment; on the other hand, she believes that much of the current stress has been foreseen and is being effectively managed. Hence the ratings of higher education debt have not substantially deteriorated. Nor does Sowder foresee future decline. The greatest number of private institutions are still rated "A" or better, and the number of "downgrades" has only "marginally" exceeded the number of "upgrades" during the last two years. Moreover, Sowder believes that higher education management will continue to effectively respond to challenges in the future.

Chapter 1

The Role of the Board

Richard Chait

Director, Center for Higher Education Governance and Leadership, and Professor, Higher Education and Management, University of Maryland

At first blush, and even upon reflection, the idea that a board of trustees could play a central role in the strategy process probably strikes many people as rather preposterous. Consider for a moment the typical board of an independent college. It has twenty-eight members and meets as a whole three or four times a year, usually for less than a day. According to the Association of Governing Boards of Universities, about 7 percent of the board's members are employed in higher education as faculty or administrators; the balance are drawn chiefly from other professions, corporations, or religious groups.

Naturally enough, the question arises whether or not a rather large, essentially lay body, meeting intermittently can or should participate meaningfully in the shaping of strategy for a fairly complex organization in a highly competitive environment. Doubtful of the board's capacity to be a major player, George Keller wondered in his pioneering book, *Academic Strategy: The Management Revolution in Higher Education*, whether boards should be involved at all in strategy formulation. Perhaps, he suggested, one or two board members might be party to "key strategy sessions"; but since most "board members are usually busy executives themselves, they often prefer to make more rapid yes-no decisions" and to leave

Portions of this chapter draw upon *The Effective Board of Trustees* (ACE/Macmillan, 1991) by Richard Chait, Barbara Taylor, and Thomas Holland. I am most grateful to my coauthors.

the details and deliberations to the president. Keller commended the idea of an annual board retreat as a "useful way of informing trustees and involving them in strategy development." Once-a-year exposure to strategy seemed just about right to him.

In examining the same issue with respect to hospitals, Andre Delbecq, former dean of the business school at Santa Clara, and Sandra Gill, president of Performance Management Resources, staked a still more controversial position. In their 1988 article "Developing Strategic Direction for Governing Boards," based on a study of boards of trustees of hospitals and boards of directors in parallel industries, they concluded that the size, composition, committee structure, and decision-making processes of traditional nonprofit boards all mitigated against effective governance—given the technical nature of health care, the confusing marketplace, unpredictable regulations, and the need to seize opportunities quickly. Instead of an unwieldy, voluntary, representational board, Delbecq and Gill recommended that hospitals establish a small strategy board comprised of five to seven compensated "seasoned industry experts" who would function as a "strategic think tank" for the chief executive officer.

> All board members would offer their best thinking and judgment; and since strategy deals with an unforeseeable future marketing risk, the board would be expected to risk giving implementation authority without requiring consensus. As such, board agendas would focus on broad environmental concerns and trends, current and potential markets, and other strategic concerns. The board should exist primarily to challenge organizational tunnel vision. The essential function of the strategic board would be to support, counsel, stimulate, and evaluate the strategy that the CEO has responsibility to implement.

The strategy board would be supplemented by an auxiliary board that would raise money and foster amicable community relations. While faintly similar to Harvard's President and Fellows/Board of overseers model, the strategy board certainly bears little resemblance to the typical college board of trustees. The case for strategy boards maintains that traditional boards are anachronisms at best, predicated on the naive assumption that full-time professionals need the wisdom of part-time amateurs in order to forge and implement corporate strategy. In truth, the argument continues, conventional boards of trustees actually impede the organization's ability to act strategically because they are too slow to respond to narrow windows of opportunity on the up side and too politically cowardly to act decisively on the down side.

These arguments cannot be summarily dismissed. Crafting and enacting an institutional strategy does indeed require a considerable, if not detailed, understanding of the enterprise, the competition, and the environment. The process also requires a substantial and sustained commitment of time.

Quite understandably, there are scholars and practitioners who believe that boards of trustees, as traditionally constituted, are not equal to the task. In addition, legions of presidents, administrators, and faculty are repeatedly warning trustees not to immerse themselves in the details of administration or curriculum. Trustees start to wonder where they fit in.

The confusion about the board's role in the strategy process stems in part from a failure to disaggregate the universe of American higher education. It is difficult, if not impossible, to generalize across the public and private sectors of higher education, from community colleges to research universities, from single institutions to multicampus systems. This essay will address primarily boards that govern single institutions, whether public or private, and also enjoy a large measure of autonomy.

In passing, however, it should be noted that the boards of state-supported colleges or state systems face formidable barriers along the path to corporate strategy. These include sunshine laws, the politics of representation, statutory and regulatory limitations on the board's latitude, too few trustees from the alumni ranks or persons with a comparable emotional attachment to the college, and disagreement among some trustees about the board's most basic roles. Is the board fundamentally the institution's guardian, the state's watchdog, the governor's emissary, the constituents' representative, or all of the above?

The second source of confusion about the trustees' role, even at independent colleges, arises from a failure to recognize that the board's principal role differs at various stages of the strategy process, which, to oversimplify, include envisioning a future, formulating strategy, implementing strategy, and monitoring progress. The process is never quite as linear as that because not all functional areas of a college or university march in lockstep. Some move forward, while others slip backward, and still others stand still. Nevertheless, I think we can profitably examine the board's role in the process stage by stage.

ENVISIONING

So much emphasis has been placed lately on the need for a vision that one might reasonably conclude that presidents are supposed to be prophets. Ordinary leadership is no longer enough; the times demand visionary, transformational leadership. Unfortunately, this burgeoning point of view, epitomized by the writings of James Fisher, appears to have impelled some presidents to withdraw to an executive aerie from which they descend a few days later with *The Vision* in hand. Other students of leadership, such as Robert Birnbaum, take the more thoughtful approach of counseling presidents to synthesize the prevalent views and ambitions of the campus community into a vision compatible with the college's culture and traditions. See where the herd's headed, in fact, and nudge them in that direction.

At this stage of the process the board is singularly equipped to make a pivotal contribution because the ablest trustees are blessed with "temporal double vision," the facility to simultaneously train one eye on the past and the other on the future. Especially on boards where alumni comprise a significant fraction of the members, trustees have a sense of the institution's history, lore, and legend. As Lawrence Butler, chairman of the Cheswick center, once noted, a board of trustees is (or should be) the organization's DNA. It carries the genetic code that transmits the institution's values, beliefs, heritage, and defining characteristics. Without being reactionaries, trustees can usefully expose campus leaders to the bedrock beneath the topsoil they turn when rethinking the institution's mission or reshaping the institution's vision.

While mindful of tradition, the effective board has the ability to foresee alternative futures precisely because it is not intimately familiar with the institution's operations and is unaware of the intricate and arcane rules that govern the academic game. The board, quite simply, is not bound by as many "givens" nor constrained by as many conventions. Just as inexperienced graduate students are often more imaginative and less cynical than seasoned administrators in analyzing case studies, I find many trustees to be remarkably inventive. On average, board members also are more familiar than academics with the environmental trends and political and economic forces that are likely to affect institutional conditions. Trustees are therefore well-situated to play a major role in envisioning an institution's future because they have a rich understanding of its past, a limited but important understanding of its present, and through their service as its unit of analysis a unique focus on the college as a whole.

At an anecdotal level I have observed several boards, working with multiconstituency task forces, contribute significantly to the envisioning process. In a typical format small groups of trustees conducted a mental tour of their campus circa 2001. At a subsequent plenary session each group reported the most tangible, visible, and palpable signs of change that they observed while "walking" around the campus. In the main, the board members' vivid and fertile imaginations both stimulated and broadened the discussion about the college's future course.

Envisioning cannot be the stuff of every board meeting or even every staff meeting. It is an activity probably best undertaken intermittently—ideally, at an extended retreat. Formulating strategy, on the other hand, is an ongoing effort. What is the board's role at this stage of the process?

FORMULATING STRATEGY

As a point of departure, it would be useful to define the concept of strategy. I am partial to a definition offered more than a decade ago by Kenneth Andrews, who was then a professor at the Harvard Business School.

> Corporate strategy is the pattern of decisions in a company that determines and reveals its objectives, purposes, or goals, produces the principal policies and plans for achieving those goals, and defines the range of business the company is to pursue . . . preferably in a way that focuses resources to convert distinctive competences into competitive advantage.

In other words, formulating strategy is the process by which an organization wrestles a vision of the future into the realm of reality. It is the act of orchestration, of harnessing the parts in a way that sums to more than the whole.

To take a concrete example, suppose an independent liberal arts college envisions a future as a genuinely and comprehensively multicultural campus. As Andrews stresses, this college must develop a pattern of policies, procedures, decisions, and actions that synergistically communicate, advance, and reinforce its chosen course. Just for starters, this requires attention to student and faculty recruitment, the nature and content of the curriculum, student and community life, financial aid policies, the role of fraternities and sororities, and the ethical dimensions of endowment investment. Clearly, the formulation of strategy is more than a weekend's worth of work. It requires the ability to link one realm of the college to another, to tie plans to budgets, to align incentives with priorities, and to match talents to tasks.

To state the case baldly, I submit that no board of trustees can do this. No governing board can, in effect, spin the intricate web that constitutes corporate strategy. This is not appropriate work for the board; this is the work the board makes certain that others get done.

The board is best positioned to ensure that management thinks strategically and devises a corporate strategy in the first instance. At a basic level the board can gauge whether the game plan contains the elements of an identifiable, consistent, competitive, and realistic strategy. Lofty but vague plans to be the finest independent undergraduate college in the region or to increase enrollments by 15 percent are aspirations, not strategies—a confusion boards can clarify. The board is also well positioned to evaluate whether the business plan makes sense, both literally (Is it understandable?) and conceptually (Is it viable?).

In formulating institutional strategy, however, the board leads largely by questions and not by answers. Through a line of inquiry common to analyzing any corporate strategy—Kenneth Andrews's classic book on the subject offers nine such questions for businesses—the board can constructively challenge the president and other campus leaders to articulate the plan clearly, to explain their reasoning persuasively, and to confront squarely the plan's feasibility, its down side, and its blind spots. In particular, the board should assess whether the plan serves the long-term welfare of the institution as a whole or the short-term indulgences of various constituents.

The board must probe respectfully but persistently. Trustees must not, as too many are, be excessively deferential. If one accepts the premise that the board cannot formulate strategy, then its responsibility to evaluate strategy assumes the utmost importance. If ever a board is to add value to the institution, this is the moment.

The same protocol, perhaps with more depth and less breadth, applies to board committees where senior staff normally present more detailed elements of the strategy for review. In actuality, such committees may be able to do more than raise questions, however valuable that service may be. At the committee level trustees can better assess the tradeoffs that proposals inevitably entail. Should we, for example, devote a still greater portion of the operating budget to financial aid in order to attract a more diverse student population? Will the abolition of fraternities and sororities enhance multiculturalism? If so, what will be the reaction from alumni diehards? Trustee committees can proliferate options and explore alternative strategies to achieve the desired vision.

I doubt, however, that a board of trustees can formulate strategy per se. Indeed, to concede that a complex and interconnected pattern of policies and practices can be forged by lay people meeting only sporadically would be to trivialize the notion of strategic planning. Earlier it was maintained that the board should play a central and active role with respect to vision and mission. By contrast, I think trustees should play an ongoing but essentially reactive role with respect to strategy formulation. Boards of trustees are not well designed to conceive, draft, or edit strategic plans. Instead, they should ask questions, examine the data, express concerns, state objections, suggest alternatives, and, when necessary, ask the CEO to return with a better plan.

IMPLEMENTING STRATEGY

Obviously, I do not regard the board of trustees as a major player in the implementation of strategy. By and large, that is the province of the administration and the faculty. The professionals must execute the strategy and manage day-to-day human, financial, and physical resources. I would like to highlight a few notable exceptions, areas where the board collectively or trustees individually might be engaged in implementation.

Independent colleges enlist trustees to raise money; and state-supported colleges enlist board members to influence the course of appropriations, legislation, and other matters of public policy. To the extent that acquisition of resources meets the definition of strategy implementation, trustees are hardly backbenchers. Furthermore, at smaller, thinly staffed colleges, trustees are often recruited to provide expertise, for example, on real estate, construction, portfolio management, and legal matters. These activities are all readily apparent examples of boards implementing strategy.

Less obviously, the board of trustees itself can be a strategic asset. Boards are apt to examine every facet of the institution except the board in terms of real or potential value added to the attainment of the corporate strategy and the overriding vision.

Let's return to the college that aspired to be a mecca of multiculturalism. How can the board, as a board, contribute to that college's comparative advantage? Of course, the board itself must be diverse in its leadership as well as in its membership. A board that has maintained open channels of communication with alumni can be deployed to try to allay the anxieties of the skeptics as the once homogeneous campus becomes more diverse. The board's commitment to the new vision could be symbolically underscored by its funding of special scholarships or through its provision of summer internships. The board could decide that all new trustees must participate in the same orientations to multiculturalism now required for all new faculty and staff. Or the trustees could develop a systematic plan to raise the board's profile, as distinct from the college's profile, within the African-American, Hispanic, and Asian-American communities.

I offer this illustration only to suggest that if charity begins at home, maybe strategy does too. The board of trustees, as an organizational entity, cannot and should not be exempt from the obligation to translate the institutional vision into a strategic game plan for the board as well as for the college's operating units. Quite the opposite, in fact, because the board should lead the way and set the pace. In that spirit, the board of one liberal arts college that just completed a year-long envisioning process may modify the trustee committee structure to reinforce the institution's newly declared priorities. Thus the board may contemplate committees on, for example, the college and the city, internationalism, and student leadership development.

With its own house in order, a board of trustees can spur the instrumental efforts of other campus constituencies with a considerably greater degree of moral authority and political legitimacy. Like other organizations, colleges sometimes need to be prodded and provoked lest the urgent drive out the important. As if afflicted with "lazy eye" syndrome, the focus of the administrators, faculty, and students can gradually, inexorably, drift toward or even sail beyond the periphery of strategy. Because the refinement and implementation of strategy requires sustained attention, boards of trustees must work to counteract this and nudge the administration every now and then to place the strategic process at the cross hairs and to keep it there.

Unfortunately, boards have an uneven record at best on this score. Of the more than 100 trustees I and my colleagues interviewed over the past four years, the majority could not recall the college's strategic priorities three years earlier, data that add credence to Delbecq's doubts about the utility of traditional boards. There are, however, some measures boards can adopt to "keep an eye on the prize," to borrow a phrase from the civil rights movement.

As a first step toward creating agendas that concentrate attention on strategy, the board, in consultation with senior staff, could develop an annual calendar or "continuous agenda" that explicitly links the work of the board and trustee committees to the college's overall strategic priorities. For each item on the agenda at a meeting of the board or one of its committees, the administration should answer in writing and in advance the question most trustees have but too few ever ask: "Why are we discussing this?" If the answer is not compelling or concerns a minor fiduciary responsibility, the board might profitably relegate the issue to a "consent agenda," which includes all routine actions that will be taken unless a trustee requests that the matter be removed from the consent agenda for board discussion.

For topics too significant to consign to the consent agenda, the CEO or the appropriate senior officer should regularly provide a precis prior to the meeting that places each agenda item in a larger, more strategic context, along with a set of questions the staff wants to raise with the board relevant to the matter at hand. This approach will help the administration and the board alike keep their eye on the target and make decisions in light of corporate strategy. For instance, a proposal before an Academic Affairs Committee to establish summa and magna cum laude graduation honors could be structured to precipitate a discussion about the requisite GPAs or about the broad range of tactics that the college might adopt to meet the strategic goal of attracting and retaining academically gifted students. The issue can be positioned as a springboard to discuss strategy or as a dead weight to mire trustees in operational details. The board bears ultimate responsibility for the choice, and its effectiveness at this stage of the process rides in no small measure on its ability to place and decide the issues that come before it within the broader framework of corporate strategy.

Boards can adopt numerous other measures to keep the institution riveted on strategy, such as prioritizing agenda items, setting time guidelines as a function of each issue's relative importance, and reserving a period at each meeting for the president to discuss what's uppermost in his or her mind. Whatever approach a board chooses, the principle remains the same. As a trustee of Williams College observed during one of our interviews, "The board has one priority: to preserve the college's clarity of purpose. There is no board agenda apart from this."

MONITORING STRATEGY

Through constant attention to strategic priorities, the board can materially influence the direction of administrative efforts. But efforts alone are not enough; there should be progress too. Nevertheless, academic administrators and board members, as a rule, appear to be more knowledgeable about efforts than about progress—measurable movement toward implementation of a strategy to achieve a vision.

We do not lack the technology to monitor progress. The Association of Governing Boards has developed extremely informative strategic performance indicators and useful constructs for comparative analyses. Projects by Kent Chabotar and Gordon Winston have yielded more pertinent financial ratios and more practical formats for boards to interpret financial performance.

Despite these advances, why does it seem that administrators and trustees are more familiar with the aspirations of their strategic plans (Oh, that's covered on page 48) than with the effects to date (Gee, I don't know)? It may be because their boards of trustees do not ask for—no, demand—the data. Trustees deliberate at length and ultimately decide major policy ques-tions, such as faculty compensation plans, tuition pricing, capital outlays, and admissions criteria—all represented at the time as essential ingredients of corporate strategy—without ever asking if, when, and how the board will know whether the policy just adopted has in fact produced the desired results.

One can easily imagine that at the college committed to multiculturalism profiled earlier, the board will learn three years from now whether or not the heterogeneity of the student body and the faculty actually increased or decreased. Data will probably be supplied about the mix of financial aid packages and the dollar volume. But at the onset of this initiative did the board ask for or did the administration offer an approach to calibrate changes in the racial climate, to estimate the degree of penetration of multiculturalism into the curriculum, or to measure the morale of faculty members from underrepresented racial and ethnic groups? Progress can, in fact, be charted through surveys, interviews, and reviews of syllabi, though these may or may not be appropriate. In fact, there may be no more critical role for the board of trustees in the strategy process than to compel the professionals to identify the most informative, most reliable indicators, however imperfect, of institutional performance, the effects of strategies, and the pace of progress toward the enactment of a vision.

Without such strategic, normative, selective, and graphic information, it will be difficult to tell if the institution is gaining or losing ground or whether anything the board or anyone else does makes a difference. Those of us who draw a salary and enjoy academic exercises may be delighted to play in a game where no one keeps score. But for trustees this could get old in a hurry. And just as William Massy recommends that institutions practice "growth by substitution," so, too, may some board members. That is, they may leave the board in favor of another activity where the fruits of their labors are more easily discerned.

But all this begs the most fundamental issue of all. Most trustees are self-lessly devoted to the betterment of the institutions they serve. Monitoring the strategy process is one of the most pivotal contributions a board can make toward that end. There may be no more effective way for a board of trustees to enable the college it governs to realize its ambitions than by insisting that its leaders keep track of the institution's progress. This is less to hold the administration's feet to the fire—though admittedly this enters into it—than to hold a mirror up to the campus community.

DOWNSIZING

If trustees vigilantly track the rate of progress toward realization of the institution's vision, the board should be able to identify performance gaps sooner and explore remedial actions earlier. In concert with the president the board could establish some "trip wires" or similar mechanisms that signal imminent financial difficulties—a task greatly simplified by the handbooks on strategic questions, indicators, and analyses published by AGB.

The board's role as sentinel assumes increased importance as more and more colleges, battered by a depressed economy and unfavorable demographics, confront the need to downsize because of financial strains. The board must be the strongest voice for fiscal prudence. In reality this means that the board has to place a governor on the motor that drives the expense side because most academics seem genetically disposed to overspend and to budget for miracles on the revenue side. Many boards are a tad too timid in this regard and approve deficit budgets that would not be tolerated in a for-profit environment.

Just as significant, perhaps only the board can prompt the faculty and staff to "think the unthinkable" and to probe explicitly the tradeoffs that academics are naturally loath to consider and quick to dismiss. Particularly during periods of financial hardship, faculty and staff prefer to make unconscious tradeoffs. For example, as even the very wealthiest institutions start to reexamine the viability of need-blind admissions, few have placed on the table a range of policy options that might preserve the principle of access. Such alternatives, which are likely to be unpopular and outlandish from the faculty's point of view, include:

- programmatic "growth by substitution"
- a higher student-faculty ratio
- fewer "boutique" electives
- a financially self-sufficient faculty club
- reconsideration of tuition subsidies for the children of faculty and senior administrators.

Like the best teachers and researchers, the best boards will challenge conventional thinking, at least occasionally.

At colleges where administrators are slow to seize the initiative, boards should direct the president to develop principles, policies, and procedures to govern retrenchment. Should the cuts be selective or across the board? Should the sanctity of tenure be preserved at all costs? Should the decision-making process be consultative and decentralized and thus inevitably protracted, or do circumstances warrant "command" decisions? These are questions that trustees should ask and administrators should answer, preferably well before the need for action arises.

The process will not, however, be entirely rational, especially in the public sector. A strategic approach relies primarily on a reasoned process informed by objective indicators of quality, centrality, and cost. Where can we eliminate weakness? Where can we add strength? How do we optimize the allocation of resources?

As a practical matter, however, politics and emotions are both powerful and influential forces, as veterans of retrenchment wars at the University of Missouri, Kansas State, SUNY, and Nebraska, among others, can attest. No sooner has a logical analysis identified a program or campus for reduction or elimination than students, faculty, alumni, legislators, and citizens, as the case may be, start to organize in opposition.

These protests so often reverse or compromise rational, defensible recommendations that one wonders whether boards and senior management, at state institutions in particular, should have a publicly available, portfolio-based strategy at all. In all too many cases the "hit list" provides the safest harbor because that status inevitably leads to a review of program quality, which indicates that the area, while not first-rate, is somewhat better than assumed and could, in fact, be top-flight with the infusion of marginal resources. In the meantime, the champions of the program or the department rally the troops to defend the territory. It may just be easier and more efficient in the long run to starve a program than to shoot it.

In any case, if a strategy has been devised and approved, the board simply must stand shoulder to shoulder with the administration in the face of a rising tide of protests. It must be unequivocally steadfast when retrenchment, authorized by the board and executed by the administration in accordance with criteria endorsed by the board, produces attacks on the institution's leaders. To do otherwise would jeopardize the presidency as well as the strategy.

CONCLUSION

I have suggested that boards of trustees should fulfill several different yet essential roles in the strategy process. During the envisioning and monitoring phases, the board should be on stage, if not always at its center. By contrast, when strategy is being formulated and implemented, the board should be off in the wings, supporting the cast and facilitating the action. In effect, boards have multiple roles: part playwright, part actor, part impresario, and sometime stagehand. To extend the metaphor a little, if the trustees find themselves with a hit on their hands—a vision that has come to life— they should be the first to lead the community in celebration. In fact, that may be one of the board's most indispensable roles; certainly it is one of the board's most delicious privileges.

Bibliography

Andrews, Kenneth. *The Concept of Corporate Strategy* (rev. ed.). Homewood, Ill.: Richard D. Irwin, 1980.

Association of Governing Boards of Universities and Colleges. *Composition of Governing Boards*. Washington, D.C.: Association of Governing Boards, 1985.

Association of Governing Boards of Universities and Colleges. *Strategic Decision Making: Key Questions and Indicators for Trustees*. Washington, D.C.: Association of Governing Boards, 1987.

Birnbaum, Robert. *How Colleges Work*. San Francisco: Jossey-Bass, 1988.

Chabotar, Kent. "Financial Ratio Analysis Comes to Nonprofits." *Journal of Higher Education*, vol. 60, no. 2 (1989), 188-208.

Chait, Richard, Thomas Holland, and Barbara Taylor. *The Effective Board of Trustees*. New York: American Council on Education/Macmillan, 1991.

Delbecq, Andre, and Sandra Gill. "Developing Strategic Direction for Governing Boards." *Hospital and Health Services Administration*, vol. 33, no. 1 (1988), 25-35.

Fisher, James L. *The Power of the Presidency*. New York: American Council on Education/Macmillan, 1984.

Keller, George. *Academic Strategy: The Management Revolution in Higher Education*. Baltimore: The Johns Hopkins University Press, 1983.

Taylor, Barbara, Joel Meyerson, Louis Morrell, and Dabney Park Jr. *Strategic Analysis: Using Comparative Data to Understand Your Institution*. Washington, D.C.: Association of Governing Boards of Colleges and Universities, 1991.

Winston, Gordon. "Organizing Economic Information for Colleges and Universities: An Alternative to Fund Accounting." Williamstown, Mass.: Williams College Project on the Economics of Higher Education, 1991.

Chapter 2

The Role of the President

Nannerl O. Keohane
President, Wellesley College

Stanford is the home terrain of the best-known university planning enterprise in the country, a true model for all higher educational institutions. At Stanford one feels rather like the guy who died and went to heaven and was told by St. Peter that each new member of the heavenly community had the right to share one story from his earthly experience with his new colleagues upon arrival. This fellow had dined out all his life on the story of having survived the Johnstown Flood, so he figured that he would tell about that great experience and really wow his audience. He proposed this to St. Peter, who did not look nearly as impressed as he had hoped, and said; "Of course, you should do as you wish; but you might want to remember that Noah will be in the audience."

Mindful that many who read this essay will be highly sophisticated educators, I thought that I would gird my loins by going back to two of the sourcebooks in higher education that I always find most stimulating: George Keller's *Academic Strategy* and Cohen and March, *Leadership and Ambiguity*. As I expected—as indeed is almost always the case—Keller provided some very useful ideas and ammunition (to which I shall return), and Cohen and March were skeptical about the entire topic, poking holes in any untoward assumption that presidents might have any significant role in planning, or indeed that planning in general is of much use at all.

I always find Cohen and March a salutary place to start for just this reason: to avoid premature delusions about the weightiness of our activities. Thus, only if statements can survive the rigorous test of refuting the skepticism of *Leadership and Ambiguity* are they worth pondering, in my view. And on this topic the hurdle of skepticism is quite formidable. *Leadership and Ambiguity* devotes only three pages to the entire topic of planning, launching it with this characteristic opening salvo: "Presidents believe in comprehensive planning, but do virtually none of it. How do we understand such an inconsistency, and what are its consequences?" (p. 114)

As evidence for this dismissive view, Cohen and March point out that presidents want to "make a mark" on our institutions: thus we "have little stake in continuity with the past," and although we may fondly hope for continuity with the future, it would be naive to expect our successors to spend much time "implementing" someone else's plan. Cohen and March go on to make the familiar point (nonetheless true for being by now a truism, and a fresher truth in 1974 when the book was written) that the *process* of planning is usually more important than the plan itself—involving an inter-action among different units of an institution, bringing people together to focus on shared interests and concerns—but rarely yielding "anything that would accurately describe the activities of a school or department beyond one or two years into the future." Mindful of this (at least at a subconscious level), busy presidents are wise enough not to spend much time on planning, despite their rhetoric.

There are several points in this trenchant analysis that I want to tease out and leave on the table as the "Cohen and March hurdle" of skepticism that any useful statements about presidents and planning will have to survive:

a) that presidents have little sense of continuity with the past, so that each presidency is an isolated moment in time, a kind of Hobbesian struggle to "make one's mark" on an institution in a fashion that will somehow survive the equally ardent efforts of one's successors to make their mark in quite a different way;

b) that in this desire to leave an imprint on the institution, savvy presidents recognize that planning for the future is of little use and thus expend our efforts elsewhere;

c) that the planning *product* seldom bears any resemblance to the future as it actually unfolds, so that even the minimal presidential effort that is warranted should be focussed on the *process* instead.

In each of these three premises it seems to me that Cohen and March are too cynical, and as a result dismiss too readily the justifications for presidential planning: and yet their cynicism spurs thought.

THE OFFICE OF THE PRESIDENT AND THE USES OF THE PAST

Let's explore a more positive approach to presidential planning and see whether it can pass the test. I hold to the old-fashioned view that thinking broadly about the course of an institution—past, present, and future—is the most important single part of a president's job; and that one's success as president—and the health of the institution one leads—depend quite a lot upon how well one performs that task.

I do not mean to suggest that "thinking broadly about the course of an institution" is exactly the same thing as strategic planning; but it is clearly the first step in that direction. It is the responsibility of the president to think as strategically as he or she can, to provide the best leadership for the institution; and the presidential office provides a unique perspective on the whole institution that is essential to good strategic planning.

Why is the president uniquely placed to think strategically? This is the beneficial side of what, from another point of view, is the hardest and most exhausting thing about the job. Presidents often lament, and with good reason, that we are in the center of all controversies, incessantly attacked by piranhas from all sides, perpetually misunderstood because we try to bring together opposed viewpoints on what the institution should be doing, pulled apart by our disparate and sometimes irreconcilable obligations to the various constituencies we must serve.

The advantage of this exposed and central location, however, is that only the president's chair provides a vantage point that includes some informed awareness of every constituency of the institution: the board of trustees, the faculty, the students, the administrators and the support staff, the alumnae, and the world outside. Presidents are themselves members of most of these constituencies—the board, the faculty, the administration, perhaps the alumnae, and most definitely, by reason of our travels and external duties, of the outside world. If we are wise and appropriately curious about the institution, we also feel some sense of identification with and appreciation for the crucial perspective of the students, the support staff, the workers in the union trades.

It is this unique situation that provides the first advantage presidents have in thinking broadly and strategically: if we are doing our job correctly, we have priceless access to all the parts of a complex institution; we feel some kinship with each one, we can understand to some degree their fears and hopes and interests, and we can try to take them into account in melding a vision that encompasses the whole.

A corollary advantage presidents have in strategic thinking, building on the first, is that by attending carefully to all this information over the course of some years, experienced presidents can build up a fund of insights, instincts, and priorities that represent distilled wisdom about the institution. Given the occupational hazards and the turnover rate in the job these days, few of us have the chance to become experienced. But it is my firm belief that successful presidents, pace Cohen and March's first skeptical hurdle, develop a strong sense of continuity with the past and future of an institution that definitely transcends one's own time in office.

A president who is truly sensitive to the various constituencies that compose a complex institution is sensitive, by the same token and almost unavoidably, to the institution's past—to those aspects of the college or university that are a legacy of its history. Even if one is not by training a historian, surely one knows instinctively that the past record of an institution is an indispensable storehouse of evidence about what is likely to be successful in the present and what will tend to fail. It is hard to imagine a thoughtful president willing to expend time and energy becoming deeply familiar with all parts of a complex institution for which one bears responsibility without also being curious about its past.

The sense of continuity that most successful presidents of established institutions feel with the past, and with their predecessors, is—like most useful insights—grounded both in idealism and in strategic shrewdness. Idealistically, most good presidents have some humbling sense of themselves as a part of a long line of leadership, stewards of the fortunes of a fragile and yet durable human enterprise. Those insignia of office that are handed to us at our inaugurations are not just so much public relations; they are powerful symbols of what our job is finally all about, and they are specifically designed to create a sense of continuity.

And in this stewardship one of the first lessons one learns—on much more strategic grounds—is that linking the present with the past in order to lay the groundwork for a positive acceptance of the future is the most powerful tool in the limited armory presidents possess. For an established institution, the most persuasive case a leader can make for a bold new step is to connect it with some widely accepted themes and images from the institution's past. This is one of our primary sources of legitimacy as leaders, and a president who remains ignorant of and unconnected with the past will almost surely fail.

This Burkean conclusion provides the surest basis for a bold and radical approach to the future. For even though presidents sometimes modestly disclaim any thought of it, Cohen and March are right: we do want to make our imprint on the institution, not just mark time and prevent disaster. Forming the habit of thinking about one's job as part of a continuum that is composed of the accreted work of people in the institution in the past—especially the work of powerful and visionary presidents—gives one a sense that it is not futile to try to make one's own mark too.

Thus this continuum rooted in the past provides the best perspective from which to think creatively about the future, to consider what kind of imprint one wishes to leave as president.

THINKING STRATEGICALLY ABOUT THE FUTURE

Having crossed Cohen and March's first skeptical hurdle, we come to the second: the skepticism about whether it is cost-effective for a busy and ambitious leader to spend time planning for the future.

Here I will deal directly with a question that I've so far begged: namely, what is the difference between *strategic* planning and any other kind of thinking about the future? And this, of course, is where George Keller's insights become most helpful. *Academic Strategy* gives a wonderful sense of what it means to think strategically: the kinds of questions one asks, the kind of mindset one cultivates and relies on.

Thinking strategically means asking what business we are really in, what this institution does (or can do) better and more distinctively than any other, what comparative advantages we have over our competitors, what we can and should aspire to be. Empowered with the kinds of unique positional insights I have sketched out earlier, the president can bring to bear both the understanding of the distinctive temper of the institution and the nature of the world in which it must compete, and he or she can use these insights to inform planning.

As Keller puts it, "A university president [must] be a manager of change, a navigator who steers his or her institution through the treacherous channels of constant transformation." (p. 123) And as anyone who has ever sailed can tell you, successful navigation requires a chart, good instruments, a destination, well-honed instincts, and a willingness to take judicious risks, as well as a seaworthy craft and a skilled and dedicated crew. With this understanding of the president-as-navigator, it is hard to see how anyone in the job could fail to spend time drawing up plans for the future. No navigator worth her salt just drifts directionless, and having a sense of direction means making carefully informed predictions about the future.

Cohen and March's abrupt dismissal of the utility of planning rests, I think, on a particular conception of what planning is about: not the kind of broad strategic navigational sense described by Keller, but a preoccupation with formalities, with abstractions, with nitty-gritty data as an end in itself. If one understands planning in this way—as a minute exercise in legislation, attempting to forecast with perfect accuracy everything that is likely to happen by gathering ever more detailed data and refining one's spreadsheets incessantly—then Cohen and March are absolutely right: no sensible president would waste his or her time in doing it.

The future (especially of messy, complex human enterprises) is inherently too unpredictable for that: it would be impossible to compile enough data or build powerful enough models to predict with a very high degree of accuracy the details of an institution's future. Our planning tools are becoming more refined each year, and we can make more and more sensible predictions; but this is not simply a matter of good tools. There is an inherent cussedness in human beings and institutions that would deliberately subvert predictions, as Dostoevsky and other astute students of human nature have reminded us. Any attempt to treat other human actors as predictable pawns in one's future plans is inevitably confounded by their inscrutable otherness and playfulness, like the flamingo croquet hoops in the game in *Through the Looking Glass* that get up and go on about their business on their own.

Sometimes, indeed, planners fall into the trap of believing they can circumvent these obstacles, as they become fascinated with finetuning the nuances of their craft and developing fancy instruments for doing so, to the point where the whole purpose of the enterprise gets lost. This is no doubt the kind of deformation *Leadership and Ambiguity* has in mind. But it is surely unwise to dismiss the utility of an enterprise just because it can go off track if one is not careful. Clearly some kinds of plans are more useful than others, and one of the most important aspects of the president's job is knowing the difference and bending the efforts of all concerned to the most useful parts of planning.

Successful strategic planning requires both sophisticated tools for amassing and massaging data and a gut instinct for direction. It requires a large dose of flexibility, humility, and a sense of humor. And no successful president can afford to do without it.

THE PROCESS AND THE PRODUCT

Does the inherent impossibility of constructing a flawless plan mean that Cohen and March's third insight is on target: that the savvy presidential planner pays much more attention to the process than the product? Here my answer would be, to some extent but not entirely so.

If the characteristic error of professional planners is to overstate their ability to predict the future in detail, the great temptation for presidential planners is to think that the measure of their success is to devise and *impose* a presidential vision for the future and then get everyone else to recognize its admirable rightfulness and just fall into line. As we all surely know by now, recognizing the admirable rightfulness in a presidential plan and falling into line is not behavior characteristic of the faculties of our institutions nor of our skilled administrative staffs. A plan cannot be just dreamed up in brilliant isolation and presented to the assembled populace; no leader since Moses on Mt. Sinai has brought that off successfully.

Instead, the successful presidential planner must give a great deal of thought to involving others in the process of planning. This is true for several different reasons. First, because, as Cohen and March make clear, the interaction in itself is fruitful for the institution: bringing thoughtful people from different constituencies together to think about the institution combats parochialness, broadens perspectives, and gives people a healthy sense of connectedness to one another. Even if no product at all emerged, therefore, this activity would have its own utility. And a president is in the best position to bring this all about.

In the second place, and equally important, involving others in the process of planning is almost sure to produce a better outcome than the isolated ruminations of even the brightest, best informed, and most dedicated leader. Aristotle, as usual, said it first: "Festivals to which many contribute are better than those which are created by a single individual." As we all know from our experience of collaborative discourse, the best ideas tend to emerge from a brainstorming session in which several people pool, test, and refine their ideas. From this dialectical experience often emerges a set of insights that are far superior to what any participant brought to the table or would ever have been able to devise alone.

To this extent the process is itself important: but it is not all-important. It is crucial to have a product, too, a sense of destination and desired outcomes and a path for getting there; and just as some destinations are more realistic and desirable than others, so some planning products are more useful and more realistic than others. This is where the involvement of the president once again becomes all-important: he or she should have a pretty clear sense of the fundamental direction from the start, not in all its outlines, but the most important points to keep in mind, and should keep the eyes of all participants focused on the final product rather than letting them get bogged down in the intricate pleasures and challenges of the process itself.

This infusion of vision, this sustained sense of desired outcomes, threading in and through the process, is the essence of presidential leadership.

THE CONTRIBUTIONS OF THE PRESIDENT IN PLANNING

With all this in mind, what are the particular contributions that a president so empowered, informed, and motivated can bring to the planning of an institution's future?

a) The president has a central responsibility, working especially with the board of trustees, to define the scope of the planning enterprise: how broadly it will be construed, whether it should include all aspects of an institution's mission or be focused more narrowly on financial planning or academic planning or planning about enrollments and student services. Identifying the issues that most need to be addressed, articulating them in a way that is easily understandable, and setting the overall tone for the planning exercise are aspects of the work that a president is (or should be) uniquely well-equipped to handle.

b) Next, working within the mandate determined by the board (which should itself bear the clear imprint of presidential purposes), the president should assemble and charge the appropriate participants and make sure they understand their goals.

In institutions such as ours, this will almost certainly involve the appointment of a planning committee or committees. It is very important to get this right, so that the committees include people who are trusted and respected by their constituencies, have the right blend of different viewpoints, are large enough to be broadly representative and small enough to be workable, and are led by those who will be good at doing so. Sometimes it will be appropriate for the president himself to take the leadership of the committees. More often, especially if the mandate is a broad one, it will be more appropriate for leadership to come from respected faculty or board members; but even so, the president must be critically involved in making these choices and ensuring the best possible guidance for the enterprise.

Successful planning must also, and equally importantly, involve the choice and empowering of effective staff to support the effort.

One of the most crucial skills a president can bring to planning is the ability to identify, recruit, and aggressively support the right people on her staff:

people who themselves have the capacity and the taste for broad institutional perspectives rather than narrow parochialism, who have some understanding of the more sophisticated tools of the planning process and the willingness to use them, who have shown some ability at foresight and are not averse to number-crunching, who get turned on by data-collecting but do not regard it as an end in itself. Failure to ensure strong staff direction is one of the commonest factors in a disappointing planning experience.

c) Next, it is the responsibility of the president to keep the whole enterprise on track: to encourage people to avoid fascinating detours, to adhere to timetables, to keep the end in view. This may sound easy, but it's not, especially when the president inevitably has other things on his mind and cannot give nearly as much time as he should to planning because of all the daily fires that must be fought and all-absorbing crises that must be overcome.

d) And then it is the job of the president to ensure that planning is communicated effectively to all parts of the college or university in appropriate ways at every stage: keeping people informed, making sure that they are genuinely consulted and not just patronized with window-dressing, sending early signals to crucial constituencies such as the board and the faculty without getting out too far ahead of the process, being mindful of less visible but powerful constituencies such as parents, alumni, or the press.

Putting it this way makes the role of the president sound too much like that of a good public affairs officer, which is indispensable, but not the same. Communication by the president is not just sharing information but getting people excited about the vision, causing them to "buy into" what is going on. This means using the priceless advantages of the bully pulpit regularly to hold out an inspiring and intriguing vision of possibilities.

e) And finally, it is the job of the president to make sure that planning is not a sterile exercise that ends abruptly when the committee makes its report. The president must ensure that embedded within the plan itself are incentives to implementation and practical ideas for doing so, benchmarks for measuring progress toward the plan, flexibility for continued planning to provide midcourse corrections as events inevitably unfold in ways different from what even the best planning effort could possibly foresee.

Here again, Keller has a crucial insight: "Planning and implementation should be concurrent, not divorced. If they are done in two entirely separate steps, plans tend to go unused by the unconvinced or wary line officers. Planning should ooze out of meetings and encounters almost unnoticed; and parts of any strategy should be championed by the very people who will need to implement it." (p. 129) From my experience at Wellesley, I would argue that this point is a particularly important insight: strategies should be formulated with the full participation of the people who must put them into practice.

Sustaining this symbiosis between ideas and implementation is one of the president's major jobs: and when this is kept in mind, the difficulty identified by Cohen and March—that no sensible president is going to spend his time implementing a predecessor's plan—is effectively avoided. Planning and implementation are not two separate, sequential things but parts of a more seamless web.

THE WELLESLEY EXPERIENCE

A brief summary of our experience at Wellesley provides a more concrete set of reference points for these generalizations.

There have been two major planning enterprises at Wellesley in my ten years as president: one in 1984–85, called the Plans and Priorities Report, and one now nearing completion, by the Committee for Wellesley in the '90s. The Plans and Priorities Committee had a relatively narrow but crucial assignment: its focus was on financial planning for the five-year period 1985–1990. The committee made the concept of "financial equilibrium" familiar at Wellesley and accomplished a number of important tasks. They gave a strong endorsement for need-blind financial aid at a time when that was beginning to have a significant impact on our budget; they emphasized the importance of several capital projects, including a hefty program of deferred maintenance, as well as major additional space and extensive renovations for both science and art, and smaller projects such as a day-care center and a new power plant.

Perhaps most important, the Plans and Priorities Committee made clear the necessity of a major capital campaign, at that time the largest ever launched by a liberal arts college, for $150 million, which we are just now successfully completing. The committee brought all constituencies of the College together in support of their priorities, including the campaign, and the Plans and Priorities Report was regularly referred to in the next five years as the Bible for Wellesley by faculty and staff alike.

The emphasis of the P&P Committee on financial planning was the direct result of our feeling—and "our" in that sentence means the leaders of the board and I, as well as the more sophisticated and knowledgeable leaders of the faculty—that Wellesley had been hurt by the absence of good planning in the 1970s. We had some financial projections from the beginning of the decade, when we celebrated our centennial; but they were ludicrously off-base in light of the double-digit inflation that was totally unexpected. We had never had an endowment spending cap and were investing for income; we had been spending a lot on program and not enough on maintenance of our buildings.

The track record of the P&P Committee was quite good: most of their projections held up impressively, and virtually all of their recommended projects have been accomplished. We found ourselves behind on faculty salaries, however, because although we met our internal goals, the competition moved up much more aggressively; and by the end of the period we had to raise tuition and fees significantly higher above inflation than P&P had projected to begin to catch up in this area. We had not realized how much maintenance was necessary in our dormitories and added a seven-year cycle of complete renovation and upgrading of our dorms to all our other capital projects. And finally—and not surprisingly—we paid far too little attention to the challenges of technology and computerization of our campus.

Despite these shortcomings, P&P is generally adjudged to have been a successful planning experience for Wellesley. Our midcourse corrections were relatively minor, and most of our purposes were achieved. This made the community amenable to another planning exercise, which indeed was demanded by the faculty, particularly as the writ of P&P ran out in 1990.

And so in the spring of 1990 we (and here the "we" is primarily the senior staff and I) began to sketch the outlines of a second planning effort that we presented to the executive committee of the board. I had initially been reluctant to launch our second major planning effort in the final intensive year of our capital campaign, feeling that for key people in our administration (and especially for me) it would not be possible to do justice to the two concurrently. I was persuaded by my staff colleagues that it was important to sustain our planning momentum and be ready to move effectively from the last year of the campaign into the postcampaign era without losing a beat. Moreover, issues such as our lagging position on faculty salaries and the challenges of enrollment in this period of demographic dearth were not going to wait until we could finish the campaign and take a deep breath. We all thought it wiser to address them within a careful planning structure.

In retrospect I think both of us were right: it's true that I have not been able to provide quite so much guidance for the C90s (Committee for Wellesley in the '90s) as I would have liked, and it has been a mighty busy year!

On the other hand, we do have a strong sense of momentum. Being aware of how crucial the campaign is as the foundation for the '90s gives a persuasive urgency to the last months of our campaign. The report of the new committee is just now being written for presentation to the board in February 1992, the month after the formal end of our campaign, so it is too early for a full assessment. But enough is clear for me to make a few comparative comments.

The Plans and Priorities Committee had been a multiconstituency committee, including six trustees, five faculty members, four administrators, and two students, plus various support and technical staff. It was ably cochaired by two financially savvy trustees (our vice chair and the treasurer) and our most respected faculty leader on financial issues. The group worked very well together, partly because the three chairs met at least fortnightly for breakfast throughout the year to chart its course and direct the research. The chair of the board and I were closely consulted, and I was an active member of the committee, but the leadership was provided by the three chairs.

The structure of C90s is much more complicated, and its charge much more complete. We have been asked to look at all parts of the institution, and to think about the decade ahead, rather than five years' worth of finances. The C90s consists of more than two dozen people, six each of trustees, faculty, and staff, plus four students and several others of us ex officio. We all believe that this is larger than optimal, and it has taken a long time for the committee to attain a sense of cohesion and common purpose; however, it serves quite well its purpose of representing all perspectives.

Because the trustee members (unlike those in the Plans and Priorities Committee) come from all over the country, not just the Boston area, the committee has not been able to meet as frequently as we should all have liked. By that same token, however, the involvement of the board in the process has been much fuller, and it is reasonable to expect the support for the final report to be all the more wholehearted. The trustee and faculty cochairs have each done a good job of communicating with the various constituencies of the college and of providing the basic direction for the group.

The C90s process has been admirably successful in what I feared would be its most cumbersome area. The parent committee has worked with great effectiveness through six task forces that were empowered to deal with particular areas in our overall planning. These task forces are more manageable in size, ten or twelve people from the faculty, students, and staff, as well as a trustee liaison who has been kept informed of the work of the task force. The task forces have addressed academic planning, administrative services, enrollment and demographics, financial planning, outreach, and student services. Their reports were presented to the C90s in June, and each report has a surprising amount of substance, bold vision, and practical common sense in its recommendations. All of us involved in the process have been impressed by this achievement.

One of the keys to this success was that for each of the task forces, the administration cochair was a member of my senior staff, who also sat as one of the administrative members of the C90s to ensure good communication. This meant that a great deal of background work and sorting out of ideas was done around our senior staff table in our weekly meetings throughout the year and most intensively at our August retreat in Maine. We were able to hone in on important issues and wrestle with them in a preliminary fashion, refine our priorities, and make sure they were addressed in the task force and in the C90s as a whole. Since each of these people is the primary implementer of the plans in each area in question, implementation is beginning before the C90s itself has even finished its report. And I'm sure that my senior staff colleagues would say that one of their main responsibilities in the process was persuading me, as president, to endorse these solutions wholeheartedly and be willing to present them to the board. Thus the close working relationship between the president and her major administrative colleagues has been shown (if anyone doubted it) to be essential to this complex planning enterprise.

The role of the faculty cochair in each case was crucial, as well, in making effective links with other faculty members and thus greatly enhancing the legitimacy of the project. The faculty cochairs worked in close harmony with their administration counterparts, which led to a new level of mutual respect across these sometimes divided constituencies. As a result, we have reached consensus on benchmarks on the stickiest of issues, including how to judge whether we have met our goal on faculty salaries.

We still have to write that report, and it will be frustrating to all of us that no single report can capture the wealth and depth of findings and recommendations of all those effective task forces, or the creativity of the vision of Wellesley in the year 2000 by members of our board at our Trustee Retreat in February. But in this case the process has indeed been a tremendously effective one. We began with the stated goal of changing Wellesley's culture from one in which faculty, students, and staff assume that we are rich enough to do anything if you just press hard enough to one that accepts the reality of limits. And amazingly enough, I think we've gone a long way toward accomplishing that goal.

We've made terms like "growth by substitution" familiar Wellesley parlance. We haven't yet persuaded the faculty to feel comfortable with the concept of "productivity"; we still call it the "p" word. But I believe we have convinced them that the faculty cannot grow, and that anything we need to do must be done with available resources, so that hard choices must be made. We've worked closely with the administrative staff to devise a plan for downsizing our professional, support, and union staff by 50–75 full-time employees without eroding our most essential services and without too much damage to staff morale. With the guidance of our Vice President for finance and administration, Will Reed, we have introduced the concept of a "core budget" to provide more flexibility in our financial planning and have developed a concrete set of benchmarks for monitoring our progress in each area.

Thanks to the extensive data presented by the Enrollment Task Force headed by Vice President for Informational Technology Peggy Plympton, we've made it clear that admissions effectiveness is Wellesley's bread and butter, and that a generous financial aid policy is essential to Wellesley's character and strength. With the leadership of our other senior administrators in academic planning, student services, and outreach, we've put forth a vision of a vibrant multicultural community and of a Wellesley that is relevant to alumnae throughout their lives.

The C90s work has been an exciting process, one that meshed unexpectedly well with our capital campaign. Now it will be fascinating to see how our planning plays out in the decade ahead, as the '90s cease to be a term of art for strategic planning and become the reality of our lives.

Chapter 3

The Role of the Chief Financial Officer

Michael Finnerty

Vice President for Finance and Administration
Yale University

As universities confront the realities of slower growth and contraction in the 1990s, campus administrators have turned more and more to long-term planning methods of dealing with their problems. One of the most vexing dilemmas they face is how to integrate effective financial planning with efforts to introduce intermediate or long-term program planning. There are two distinct realities within higher education. The first is that the highly decentralized nature of the academic program has always made prospective long-term planning extremely difficult if not impossible. This fact has traditionally been reinforced by a healthy skepticism on the part of academics about an institution's ability to project and predict the shape and direction of its academic programs. The second reality is that long-term planning has long been a valued and effective tool for finance professionals and has been advocated by finance offices on most university campuses for some time.

The general relationship between program and finance has been characterized by tensions stemming from the fact that financial operations are centralized whereas academic program structure is essentially decentralized. All too often this has led to a perception that the role of the finance office has been to constrain both the growth of programs and improvements in their quality. To overcome such misperceptions, the finance office must reconstruct its relationship to the academic programs to help academic leaders understand the true nature of the resources available to them, then encourage those leaders to use the analytical and planning skills available within the finance office as a means of supporting and protecting academic program quality in today's constrained environment.

This chapter is based solely on my personal experience with the planning process as it has evolved at Yale University. I do not attempt to survey the very extensive literature on strategic planning, either generally or within higher education, nor to compare or analyze that process in the industry as a whole, as I have had little experience with it outside my own university. My purpose is to provide a perspective from one who has served as chief financial officer at a comprehensive research university during a period when that university ventured into a more formalized planning process than had ever previously been attempted. My hope is that a description of my own experiences may stimulate useful discussion of how university chief financial officers and finance offices can be most effective in aiding this process.

THE PLANNING PROCESS

The roots of Yale's current planning effort go back to the mid-1980s when, having only recently achieved a few years of recurring operating budget balance, the university was at last in a position to address a backlog of long-deferred investments in facilities. At the request of the board of trustees, the provost, working with the financial staff, undertook a preliminary five-year review of the financial outlook for the university, with the aim of establishing what financial resources might be available for reinvestment in the physical plant. This effort was in part motivated by the board's desire to provide some analytical framework for defining the university's debt capacity. Tax-exempt borrowings had been the primary financial resource for the proposed capital reinvestment program. This initial effort largely assumed a status quo program. It relied on fundamental elements of financial planning to project the resources available over a defined time period, it identified those that were already committed to maintenance of the existing capital reinvestment program, and it hoped to find a resource increment that could be made available to launch a more concentrated attack on Yale's building problems.

Following the presentation of this information to the board, it was agreed that it should be used to begin a universitywide assessment of precisely which capital needs were the highest priority. The provost commissioned a campuswide planning effort to define the pent up building demand. Two specific requirements identified by the financial planning review were imposed: projects to be considered had to be achievable within a five-year period and had to be within the constraints of the status quo financial projection.

A Building Assessment and Development Plan

The provost's first act was to appoint a planning group to undertake a building assessment, which was a community-based assessment of building needs viewed from the bottom up. Over sixty senior faculty and administrators from all over the university community were assigned either to an overall capital planning committee or to one of four subcommittees tasked to assess specific building needs under programmatically based groupings: scientific facilities, other academic facilities, residential facilities, and campus infrastructure. Attempts were made to have faculty and administrators review building demands across and outside their program areas. The scientists were involved in assessing undergraduate residential facilities, while central administrators would be looking at the needs for academic program space, and so on. This process was designed to look at the program demands and roll them up into an overall campus need.

Each department on campus was asked to submit its own perception of the facilities it needed for its program for review by the appropriate committee. At the same time, an engineering firm was retained to conduct a bottom-up analysis from a different perspective. Each individual campus building was surveyed in turn, without consideration of the particular program it was being used for to define the building's own specific needs, such as electrical systems, air-handling systems, health and safety code improvements, moisture protection, and other elements that would be essential in terms of its maintenance as an asset.

All the information produced by these two bottom-up processes was accumulated and reviewed by the appropriate subcommittees, then integrated by the campuswide planning committee into a document presented to the board. This final document represented the administration's view of how much capital improvement could be accomplished with the funds available over a period specifically limited to five years.

The initial financial building generated yet another planning review, which was far more narrowly based and centralized. We looked at our overall university development effort to assess what role it could play in addressing the backlog of building investment needs and in minimizing the impact of this demand on our ongoing operating resources. This review focused on two questions:

1. How could fund-raising efforts be best targeted to address the need for more facilities (which was emerging as one of the most critical needs on campus)?

2. Should this fund-raising effort be consolidated into a universitywide fund-raising campaign?

After more than a year of concentrated work throughout the community on these two planning processes, presentations were made to the board on the conclusions of each one. A facilities-renewal program estimated to cost roughly $500 million over a five-year period was presented. The program reflected the priorities as identified at the departmental level and as reviewed by the campuswide efforts. The conclusion of the development planning review was that both the significant increase in fund-raising that would be required by the $500 million program and the need to redirect development targets away from traditional endowment resources toward gifts that could be expended directly on facilities could best be given focus through a universitywide campaign.

The board's response to these three early elements of the planning process was enthusiastic. This more formalized approach to multiyear planning resembled the kind of process board members were familiar with in their own business experiences, and it held a great attraction for them. They had never been fully comfortable with the campus's highly decentralized annual incremental approach to both financial and program management concerns. Not surprisingly, they called for more planning, in a more in-depth way, and over a far more extended time frame. Three follow-up planning efforts were commissioned.

Expanding the Plan

All of the activity thus far had been to answer the question of how to identify incremental resources the university could apply to the huge backlog of capital investments in its physical plant without undermining its academic program. The board now wanted the premise of the capital plan it had just received radically expanded. The university's officers were asked to revisit the question of facilities demand, eliminating the two constraining elements previously imposed. The university's officers were asked to produce a facilities plan without any limitation either on funds available or on the time period over which actual construction might occur. It was the board's feeling that by limiting the bottom-up review of both program and engineering demands to those resources already identified, the true facilities demand was obscured. The officers, notably the provost, argued that to undertake such an unconstrained view of "facilities demand" would be counterproductive in that it would inevitably define a demand that was unachievable, either because of the enormous resources it would consume or simply because we could not mount such a massive construction program without having to close down the ongoing academic program. They pointed out that spending a great deal of time working with the academic community to identify such a program would do more harm than good because it would raise expectations that they would never hope to fulfill.

The board's response was that the initial request for facilities needs from all of the program elements had provided the basic data needed to expand the plan so that the broader community did not need to be involved any further in presenting that information. But board members insisted that it was critically important to define the entire facilities demand as developed through the bottom-up planning process. Only in this way, they felt, could we make as definite a decision about what we could not do as we were making about what we intended to do in the near term. Thus a second, far more centrally controlled facilities planning effort was undertaken to review in the broadest possible sense what would be required to restore the existing physical plant to university standards of functionality and to provide new facilities and improvements in anticipation of future program changes over the years.

The next steps identified for the development effort were much more operational and more consistent with traditional university approaches. The five-year financial plan and the assessment of the unmet building-investment needs both established that there would have to be a significant effort to increase fund-raising as part of the program for reinvestment. Otherwise the building demands would inevitably undermine the fundamental academic program. More specifically, it was clear to those involved in the development effort, as well as to the board, that the redirection of fund-raising activities toward expendable facilities gifts for existing rather than new facilities would require a significant reeducation process both on campus and with the alumni. The message and objectives needed to be stated consistently throughout the various schools as well as to alumni groups, and the best way to accomplish this would be through a coordinated, universitywide fund-raising campaign. Those involved in development planning were asked to take their efforts a step further—to design the actual conduct of such a campaign and to make a more sophisticated assessment of how much potential existed for increasing the overall level of university gifts and, more significantly, to estimate the likelihood of redirecting those gifts toward investment in the university's existing, aging physical plant.

An Academic Plan

The board also concluded that the recommendations of the three planning efforts undertaken thus far—the multiyear look at financial resources, the assessment of the inescapable demand for reinvestment in an aging physical plant, and the need for expansion and redirection of fund-raising efforts—could not be properly pursued without a similar long-term look at the direction and needs of the academic program.

Much debate ensued. Such tangible needs as the structural and engineering requirements of campus facilities, economic estimates of identifiable sources of university revenue, and marketing appraisals of potentials for fund-raising did not differ greatly from the elements of a business plan in a commercial organization and lent themselves readily to quantitative analysis and projections. The highly decentralized scholarly process of a university was another matter altogether. Any attempt to centrally define specific academic program goals and objectives would be considered quite at variance with the fundamental character of a university. The evolution of the various and disparate academic programs on a campus is organic in nature, resulting from the frequently unplanned activities of thousands of individual scholars, faculty, and students. How, then, could the administration presume to put together for the board a central concept for the future of Yale's academic program that would define future demands specifically enough to facilitate the development of a discrete facilities plan and the establishment of particular fund-raising program targets?

But there was no avoiding the central point of the board's concern. Where would the board and the administration be if after five to ten years of massive investment in facilities and an intensive fund-raising effort with the alumni and others supporters, the university found itself with a physical plant and a financial structure that did not support the academic program as it might exist?

It was agreed that we would undertake to define the academic needs of the university, but with the proviso that while the process was intended as counterpoint to the physical and fiscal planning done thus far, it would not be done in as regimented or centralized a manner as in the previous efforts.

Second-stage planning. The provost requested each department chairman, each dean, and the director of each significant universitywide academic support program to work with their faculties and staff to define a broad academic program strategy without being concerned about specific sources of funding to support change or questioning how one might restructure existing resources to accomplish change. Little specific quantitative backup or analysis was requested, and in most cases little was provided. But the effort did produce an attempt by each of the individual program units to define for itself where it thought scholarly activity in its field was headed and what its department or school would need to look like in the future to continue to meet the standards of excellence for which the university stood.

The provost then worked with the deans, directors, and chairmen to fashion these statements into a very broad, nonprescriptive presentation to the board of an overall institutional academic strategy that was truly a compilation of a highly decentralized, subjective vision of academic program directions. In response to the board's desire for yet a different mode of "unconstrained demand assessment," this effort was conducted with almost no attention to either the facilities for or financial aspects of such strategies.

As each of these second-stage plans was initiated, the board also directed the provost and the vice president for finance and administration to begin working on a far more sophisticated and detailed assessment of the earlier financial plan. The analytical framework was extended to a ten-year period; and for certain elements such as endowment and debt capacity, the horizon was extended to fifty years. This in-depth planning effort had two objectives:

1. To provide a far greater level of confidence in the underlying financial projections that had been done in the original financial overview.
2. To serve as a sound financial projection that would ultimately be used to apply realistic constraints to the program choices being developed in both the academic strategy and the facilities demand assessment.

To accomplish these ends, the planning effort was broadened to include the financial offices throughout the campus, mirroring the bottom-up nature of the process used for the initial facilities review and academic strategies development. Those responsible for managing individual programs were asked to make assessments of the following:

- the availability of grant and contract income,
- managing clinical income,
- maximization of auxiliary services income,
- trends in enrollment versus tuition pricing models.

This information made it possible to compile detailed background papers on the complex financial structures in the university environment as well as realistic assessments of both the revenue- and expense-based trends over the decade. All of these planning and analytical efforts were overseen and brought together by the finance office in a very detailed university financial plan. That plan could be compared to the hopes and dreams expressed in the "unconstrained" facilities and academic plans.

An Integrated University Plan

Once the three second-stage planning efforts were complete, the university administration, working with the board and the various leaders of the academic programs and administrative units on campus, began the development of what, we hope, will become a university plan that successfully integrates financial, academic, and facilities needs and realistic constraints. Now that these elements have been brought together, the entire university community is in the process of trying to make clear choices within the unconstrained facilities plan and the unconstrained academic strategy, as well as between the two plans. This process intimately involves the central offices responsible for the management of university finance and the preservation of its facilities assets, and the decentralized academic leadership that is responsible for the quality and scope of the academic program. Their choices will reflect what we hope to accomplish and a much clearer understanding of what is not possible. The final results will be embodied in a specific set of financial, facilities, fund-raising, and academic objectives. This will integrate the plans developed by every individual academic program and administrative unit, all of which have evolved with continual feedback from the centralized elements of the various planning efforts over the past four years.

When we began these processes five years ago, no one had any notion that we would develop a "Strategic Plan for Yale University." And in fact, when the process of making our aspirations fit into our thoughtfully analyzed financial constraints is finally completed, I do not believe we will even then have a strategic plan in the traditional sense. We will, however, have undertaken most of the steps that are involved in a traditional strategic planning process. Certainly, at the very least, we will have a tactical plan for the university's next decade that is informed by, guided by, and constrained by strategic analysis and planning done within the variety of independent elements that make up the university's unique structure.

ANALYSIS OF THE PROCESS

Looking back on this five-year-long process, it would be easy to characterize it in ways suggesting that many tenets of good planning have been ignored. For example, there was never any effort at the outset to define the ultimate outcome of the process as a comprehensive university plan. There was no initial attempt by leadership to think through and define broad institutional missions that could then inform the strategic planning process within the individual units. The process was initiated on the more traditional university assumption that what we have is good and should be preserved, and that the real question is how best to continually improve and add to it within the resources we already have.

The entire process was in fact reactive as opposed to proactive. Rather than attempting to develop a strategic plan or anticipating institutional directions and missions for the future, the university initiated the process of financial and facilities planning entirely in response to specific problems that had evolved. It was less a question of defining Yale's future shape and direction than an attempt to analyze and understand specific current problems in the context of the future. Even more significantly, not one of the elements at the core of the academic program or the university's value system was included in the precipitating events that spurred the early planning processes. Deferred maintenance needs, crumbling physical plant, shortfalls in outside income, escalating fringe benefit rates, and so on were the elements and pressures that led the university to take a longer-term perspective in looking at its financial, facilities, and academic programs; none of them is involved in academic program definition. It was only after investigation of these elements that the university began to bring in the question of the shape and scope of the academic program in the context of the problems we were facing.

Degrees of Guidance

Ideally, as a strategic plan process goes forward, any institution would like to involve its community in the planning and decision-making process as broadly as possible. However, the several interrelated but independent planning processes that have gone on at Yale over the past several years have involved the broader community only sporadically, in discrete elements. Only the board and a small group of senior management have been cognizant of all elements of each process and have been involved in the process as a whole throughout the period. The current activity of integrating individual plans with universitywide constraints is the sole process that has had consistent, broad-based input from the entire community.

The individual program and organizational plans that were required as part of the various planning processes were developed with little guidance and specific direction from senior management at the outset. This was particularly true of the elements of the planning process that were most important to the university's future: the academic programs and the academic program facilities demand. These elements were specifically elicited through a process that offered the individual participants nearly complete freedom in defining their needs and stating their goals and objectives.

Vastly different degrees of analytic discipline were applied to the development of various aspects of the plans. While traditional, detailed rigor was involved in financial estimating, engineering analyses of individual buildings, and realistic assessments of fund-raising potentials, no such analytic evaluation was requested or desired with respect to the intuitive judgments provided by the academic leaders about the future direction or shape of individual programs.

One could define many other "weaknesses" in Yale's iterative evolutionary planning process, but that is not the point. The weaknesses I've just mentioned reflect the dilemma inherent in undertaking broad institutional planning at a comprehensive research university. Most people would agree that for institutional strategic planning to be effective, it should be comprehensive and encompass all elements of the institution's activities and mission. Yet the very nature of a university is that individual program units, even individual scholars, prize and demand a great deal of autonomy and freedom in pursuit of their objectives. The process at Yale, I believe, was well suited to solving the tension between the need at an institutional level to conserve resources in order to insure the long-term viability of the programs and the fundamental character of a research and scholarship program dependent on a high degree of small-unit autonomy and a great deal of freedom in decentralized decision making.

The process as it evolved—specifically because it was not comprehensive in nature at the outset—allowed each of the various planning elements to be conducted in a manner that reinforced decentralized academic program decision making while providing vigorous institutional discipline in assessing realistic long-term resources available to the programs. As we now go through the process of bringing these various elements together into an integrated university plan, we hope to achieve one that will be simultaneously developed from top-down and bottom-up perspectives. Such a plan should contain sufficient flexibility to slip past overly constraining individual academicians and still provide the board and senior administrators with a functional means of monitoring their long-term responsibility for preserving Yale's program.

THE ROLE OF THE CFO AND FINANCE OFFICE

My experience over the past five years, particularly as we move through the difficult maneuver of pulling the various plans together into a single strategic plan for Yale, has reinforced my view that the chief financial officer, and more generally the finance office, has an absolutely critical role to play in strategic planning at any higher education institution. It has also convinced me that that role can easily be nullified if it is undertaken without a clear understanding of the special characteristics of a university environment and of some of the very real distinctions between planning in such an environment and planning in other institutional environments, such as commercial enterprises and governments.

The chief financial officer and the finance office need to understand that while the university is, in fact, a corporate body, few of its functions are institutionwide in nature, and those that are will not be the central program clients. The functions that most lend themselves to institutional thinking are the ones that are also most likely to have a heavy financial office involvement—such issues as preservation of assets, both financial and physical, establishment of systems of internal controls, implementation of the board's and the officers' fiduciary responsibilities, reporting financial information to external review bodies, and so on. The most important program elements are not managed on a universitywide basis, and each one clings with fervor to its autonomy and bottom-up decision-making processes.

It is important to recognize up front that in the case of not-for-profit institutions of higher education, none of the principal institutional goals or objectives is ever likely to be stated in financial terms (in direct contrast to what might be expected from either commercial or government entities). This distinction is critical for the finance office, since higher education looks frequently to the business or government sectors for role models in strategic planning processes. A profit-making firm is likely to establish such things as profit margin or return on investment as key objectives, while government might well state its overriding objectives in terms of reduction of tax burden or income redistribution. These are all financial concepts. The primary objectives for a not-for-profit educational institution, however, are programmatic in nature. This means that the role of the finance office in the institutional planning process is likely to be less central, though not necessarily less important, than it might be in either a government or commercial firm. If that is recognized, the input from the financial office can be maximized; if it is not, there can be conflict with the academic leadership.

"Who is the chief financial officer anyway?"—another interesting question to be thought through in terms of the institutional character of a university. The answer is not only important for the finance office, which needs to understand its role in the planning process with the internal community, but it also needs to be well understood by the board and others who may have to oversee the process. Typically, the traditional responsibilities of a chief financial officer do not only reside in the person titled vice president for finance or something similar; several important areas, such as resource allocation, reside with the chief academic officer. For the finance office to play a significant role in the planning effort, it must play its part in direct partnership with the academic leadership's financial responsibilities, not in competition with them. Otherwise it will be kept from involvement in the fundamental program and financial analysis that is essential as the various planning efforts are brought together into an institutional plan.

All of these can be easily dealt with if the chief financial officer begins the process by making sure the finance staff understands the primary objectives of the finance office in a not-for-profit educational environment. If the finance office staff views its role within the institution as being to monitor, control, and minimize expenditures, staff members are not likely to be invited to important conversations about program choices and trade-offs. However, if everyone in the office understands that its role is to responsibly finance the maximum direct program activity possible, the office is likely to be viewed as an ally of the academic leadership and invited in. This does not relieve the finance office of its traditional role as a fiduciary for current assets or its responsibility to provide a stable, long-term financial underpinning for programs. But it will help staff members become more creative in finding ways to minimize institutional liabilities by maximizing the proportion of current resources for existing or new programs.

Inherent Problems

Among the most difficult problems for university finance officers is finding ways to reinforce program autonomy while satisfying the need to aggregate financial information on a universitywide basis and to report it accurately and with discipline to external entities. A simple solution is to provide highly centralized and relatively inflexible financial reporting in management techniques that insure the comparability of information being aggregated. However, these are frequently at odds with the notion of decentralized decision making in the academic environment. It is far more difficult, but in the long run more productive, to find other means of aggregating the same information in ways that reinforce the process by which academic decisions are made.

Full participation in the planning process may require finance professionals to accept a certain degree of professional frustration. The finance office is frequently evaluated on its ability to pull together accurate, comprehensive financial reporting and planning for external audiences that want to feel comfortable with this information while simultaneously placing great stock in it. These requests are judged in part on highly organized internal consistency, uniform standards for data and analysis, and overly neat "cross-footing" to a balanced product. However, to be fully engaged in the development of an academic rather than a financial strategy, the financial staff also has to become comfortable working within a highly decentralized environment in which many individual decisions are made without respect to overall institutional constraints. This rarely leads to a crisp document with a clear conclusion.

The need to perform well in both environments presents the finance office staff with their greatest challenge. They must find a way of bringing to bear for the academic leadership—whether president, provost, or board—legitimate institutional resource constraints that will define the size and scope of the academic program without interfering with that leadership's responsibility to generate specific program decisions.

In addition, the professional staff in the finance office must understand that their natural affinity for quantitative analysis and organized planning is not likely to be shared by administrators in academic or support units, particularly those in the smaller programs. But it is also extremely unlikely that the administrators and academic leaders in those units will feel comfortable in calling upon a central office of financial professionals to do the analysis and presentation for them, unless those professionals are seen not as agents of central control but as a valuable resource in assisting academic units to do their planning and analysis. When long-term planning and even central resource allocation decisions are rarely initiated in university environment other than at times of financial constraint, it is a difficult task for finance professionals to convince the community that they are there, in fact, to maximize the resources available to direct program spending. However, I believe this concept is the most critical of all to the finance office's potential role and success in the planning process. If that role is confined to setting limits on the horizons of the academic programs, finance professionals will be seen as critics rather than as full partners in a process whose outcome is intended to preserve and enhance the quality of those same academic programs.

THE REWARDS OF EVOLUTION

I believe that the iterative and evolutionary planning process that has come about at Yale has been successful, in part, precisely because we did not set out with the notion of creating either a strategic institutional plan or even any element of an academic plan. The work undertaken by the finance and building service units in the early years was viewed as supportive of the academic program and goals. As the process evolved to asking the academic leaders to do their own program planning, the information from the earlier efforts was available for them to use to support their thinking; it did not dictate it. When the level of planning was intensified in response to the board's request, there was a common understanding of the fundamental problems that had been uncovered in the early stages by both the academic leadership and the central administrative leadership.

The true test of this integration is now under way as we pull together all of these efforts into a single plan in which "real world" constraints on university finances are coming into direct conflict with the academic vision of the program leaders. It is to be hoped that our earlier efforts have shown academic leaders the valuable support units such as finance, building service, and development can offer them in the planning process. Equally, for those who lead administrative support units, these early efforts will have reinforced the conviction that a university plan must always begin with an academic goal, not a financial one. This partnership and understanding of each other's roles in essential. Failure to achieve it results only in the dismal, traditional university stereotypes: financial administrators viewing academic planning as nonquantitative, nonanalytical, and devoid of real-world constraints; academic leaders viewing financial staffs as overcentralized number crunchers and bean counters with no idea what research, scholarship, and teaching are all about.

The most important element in both sides' understanding the need for this vital partnership is the recognition that the true value of planning lies in the interactions it forces and fosters—inevitably, any plan may well be out of date the day after it is adopted. In the end, the primary purpose of a plan is to provide a yardstick by which both the academic and financial leadership of an institution will know for sure when the world has changed on them.

Chapter 4

The Michigan Experience

Gilbert R. Whitaker Jr.

Provost and Vice President for Academic Affairs
University of Michigan

Planning for change in a large organization where legitimate desires and aspirations always exceed revenues by very large amounts is difficult indeed. Where revenue growth occurs, only small changes can be funded and where revenue falls, nothing can be cut—even though something must.

Fourteen years ago, during my first year as dean of the School of Business Administration, Harold Shapiro was the provost—the university's chief academic officer and chief budget officer. He created something he called a "priority fund." To accomplish this he took one percent off the budget of each unit, which gave him discretionary money to reallocate to those areas he determined had the highest priority. Before procedure could be repeated, however, Shapiro became president of the university, Michigan's economy collapsed, and our appropriation was slashed. As a result, everyone's budget was reduced six percent, and nothing was left to be reallocated.

That was followed by additional reductions, high inflation, and continuing shortfalls. Billy Frye, our then provost, began a review of three schools for possible major budget reductions. All three had suffered major enrollment declines and were viewed as relatively low-quality performers. This very painful, very public process resulted in significant reductions for these colleges spread over time. But in the aggregate few dollars were recaptured.

More recently, when James Duderstadt, our current president, became provost in 1986, he began a major strategic planning process among the schools and colleges and reinstituted a priority fund-reallocation mechanism. Again, funds were taken off the top, making them available for reallocation to priorities identified through the strategic planning process. Results of this planning process were uneven, however, because some units did an excellent job while others never came to grips with the issues. Unfortunately, most of the "off-the-top" funds were used to fund basic salary programs, leaving little or nothing for focused reallocation toward university priorities. A notable exception was our Target of Opportunity Program for recruiting minority faculty to Michigan, which has been very successful.

This quick sketch does not articulate the hard work and valiant efforts that went into the priority decision process of the past. The subject of this chapter is current planning efforts at Michigan, where we are stepping forward on several fronts to address our funding needs for new ventures.

COSTS AND REVENUES IN HIGHER EDUCATION

In early 1989 Charles Vest, my predecessor as provost, asked me to chair a task force on costs in higher education, set up in part as a reaction to requests from our board of regents and in part from the wish of both president and provost that these issues be seriously considered. Although the task force's charge was to look at costs, we felt compelled also to consider revenues. We felt that an evaluation of costs alone, without some compelling threat of reduced revenue growth, would not be viewed as credible by the university community.

As a public university, our revenue sources are multiple: state appropriation, tuition, research grants, contracts (largely federal), and gifts and income from endowment. A careful review of each of these sources suggested to us that growth in revenues would be extremely slow over the next several years and that funds for new initiatives would have to come both from revenue increases and from cost containment or cost reduction.

The task force's report, "Enhancing Quality in an Era of Resource Constraints," was submitted in March 1990, though its public release did not occur until July 1990, when Provost Vest announced his intention to accept the presidency of MIT. So as fate would have it, I ended up as provost with my own report on my desk for consideration. Had I known how the world would change around me, that report might have been very different. By July 1990 it was unfortunately becoming clear that our revenue projections were being fulfilled, and we were going to have to live with the "revenue diet" that the report forecast. The university budget allowed for an average budget increase of 2.6 percent across all of the budget units, with a few special allocations based on a variety of different circumstances. These ranged from special tuition increases to unrestricted budget additions to our largest units. No one was at all happy, and prospects were (and remain) dim for major revenue gains.

In 1991 we initiated a wide variety of efforts to restructure our budgeting and planning processes and to reduce costs. These efforts included:

- Consulting with several other universities.
- Appointing a task force (PACE—Provost's Advisory Committee on Excellence in an Era of Revenue Constraints).
- Taking our first real universitywide steps toward enrollment planning by units and by programs.
- Implementing an annual budget with differential allocations and special revenue enhancements.
- Discussing changes in methods of managing space utilization.
- Asking all units to plan for the possibility of a two percent base reduction during the current fiscal year in preparation for possible executive order rollbacks or loss of indirect cost recovery funds.
- Beginning a universitywide total quality management program.

Two ongoing faculty committees—the Committee on the Economic Status of the Faculty and the Budget Priorities Committee—also provide advice and guidance on budget issues.

Clearly, each of these activities has different degrees of importance for planning and managing the institution. Many sound as if we should have been doing them for years. Those that may appear the most routine, however, may well be the most valuable for controlling revenue or expenses at Michigan, so I will attempt to forecast where each is headed and try to estimate its importance to our future.

Enhancing Quality in an Era of Resource Constraints

Because the report of the Task Force on Costs in Higher Education outlines most of Michigan's current efforts to plan for a revenue-constrained future, what follows is a brief summary of its findings and suggestions for dealing with cost and revenue issues.

With the advantage of hindsight and the sobering effect of being the receiver of the report, the major change I would make in it would be a more creative translation of its business language to a more acceptable academic language. Indeed, our current quality-program design team is hard at work on this task. However, the language itself probably helped to focus attention on the report. The report suggests some major cultural changes in the way we carry out our tasks:

- Innovation by substitution, not growth by incremental resources, will have to become the operative management philosophy.
- Individual units, as well as the central administration, begin an ongoing process of evaluating the way decisions are made, from the lowest possible level upward, to ensure the fact-based, customer-oriented decision making that is consistent with their organizational missions and goals.
- The leaders of the university and its individual units must make quality the centerpiece of their institutional strategy. Quality must undergo a transformation of meaning in the minds of these leaders and the members of the university community alike. It must go from meaning "more and better of everything" (with all the resource requirements that implies) to "being the best in what we choose to do" (not everything) and "searching relentlessly for means of improving quality that reduce cost or are cost neutral or low cost in character."

These broad cultural changes were viewed as a necessary condition for what the report terms "excellence on a revenue diet," the collection of activities we are undertaking to adjust to our realization of the circumstances we face. These cultural changes also have important implications for budget planning and operating the university. Some of the changes we anticipated include the following:

- Many administrative and bureaucratic rules and regulations will be eliminated without any negative effects after a regular review focusing on their relationship to quality and cost of operations.
- Many administrative activities in academic and support units will be eliminated when their necessity and performance is evaluated in the light of service to customers.
- Internal support and service activities will be delivered in a wider variety of ways, with additional management responsibility being assigned to the users and recipients of the services.
- Faculty workloads will become more flexible and individualized, differing between and among units, over the spectrum of an individual's career. Faculty participation in the determination of such workloads will become more extensive.
- New programs will be developed and offered in the summer and at other times to generate incremental revenues.
- Enrollment management and its relationship to unit financial re-

sources will become a more significant factor in the evaluation of long-term budget issues.

These changes will not be easy to achieve, nor will they occur at the same time. We all know, for example, that changes in the ways we define faculty workloads and reward faculty are very difficult to accomplish. Our budget problems may be difficult, but it appears we do have time to make adjustments. If our problems do not become too severe, our rather slow, cumbersome, consultative processes will serve us well. If the situation should suddenly worsen, more dramatic actions may be necessary.

Consultation with Other Universities

During the 1990–91 academic year Tim Warner, associate vice president and director of budgets from Stanford, John Curry, vice president of budgeting and planning from the University of Southern California, and Clinton Sidle, director of institutional planning and research from Cornell, were among several visitors who spent a day or more on campus to discuss their institution's approaches to their own major budget issues. In each case they met with representatives of the committees mentioned above, the university executive officers, and others. We learned a great deal, but we didn't find the "silver bullet" for Michigan. The struggle continues to find ways to improve our ability to budget, plan, control, and spend; but we have found a number of useful ideas to help us with our problems, and we intend to keep on with these kinds of activities.

PACE

The PACE task force was appointed to deal with both short- and long-term budget issues. As it turns out, the group's attention has been focused primarily on long-term issues, which has meant, in turn, that annual budget issues have been the chief consideration for our ongoing Budget Priorities Committee, along with the long-term consequences of short-term issues. Because of some overlapping memberships in the two groups, the dual structure seems to be working out reasonably well.

Our current budgeting and accounting practices leave much to be desired in terms of informed decision-making on financial matters. General-fund unit budgets are largely related to personnel, current accounts, and financial aid, and no units are charged for any central services, including space. Indeed, only in the last several years have fringe benefits been charged to the units. Non-general-fund units have a variety of practices with regard to budgeting. Annual budgets in all units chiefly involve changes at the margin in expenditure accounts, with revenue budgeting and revenue responsibility borne centrally. Thus general-fund budgets are cost-center budgets but do not include all costs attributable to each individual unit.

These current budget practices have led PACE to investigate methods of more direct attribution and allocation of all costs attributable to a unit as well as to exploring ways of attributing revenues. Most of our work to date has focused on the academic units. The approach chosen is known as conscious net support (CNS). While a variant of this approach has probably been used for years, it has been based more on intuition than on a precise understanding of the financial facts. Under the proposed CNS approach, the net financial support received by a unit is computed and debated in the context of its priority before a budget is set up. Improvement in the data and in understanding will, in theory, improve the process.

At Michigan both revenue and cost attribution are difficult to assess. The amount of actual revenue is confused by our two-tier multirate tuition structure in which rates differ across units and on the basis of Michigan residency. The latter difference is difficult to deal with because units are not totally free to determine the resident/nonresident mix since the legislature has established a percentage guideline for undergraduates of 70/30. In addition, a number of long-standing informal agreements concerning residency are in place for the various schools and programs. As a first step, PACE has attributed all tuition revenue as if all students were paying the nonresident tuition charged by their program. This method allocates much of the state appropriation to the individual units.

Originally the CNS model approach was presented to the deans without numbers, and considerable discussion ensued, which escalated enormously once numbers were attached to both revenues and costs. Almost every unit had suggestions for improvement, and several rejected the entire notion of presenting such information, believing that any real understanding of "net support" by a unit could lead to poor assessments of quality or centrality unduly influenced by the numbers.

Numerical outcomes produced some surprises—primarily the clear realization that much of the net subsidy flowed from our largest unit, the College of Literature, Science, and the Arts (LS&A), to other units. Several units were net providers under the revenue models used. (Because the central library was treated as an academic unit, its expenditures were not allocated to the units.)

We have not so far been able to devise a specific formulation on how to determine the appropriateness of the net support indicated by the accounting formulation, though it has led us to undertake additional work dealing with the underlying drivers of costs and revenues (see below). By and large, the units seem willing to allow the provost to make decisions about net support while reserving the right to complain bitterly about individual outcomes.

Enrollment Management

It is fair to say that overall enrollment at Michigan has been largely unmanaged, even though total enrollment has varied little for the past fifteen years. Some unexplained force has resulted in relatively constant total numbers, though with a considerably changed mix of students. Because of our variable rates, reserves have fluctuated along with the mix, producing some unpleasant surprises as actual results have diverged from those that were budgeted. Attention at the central level has been primarily devoted to new freshmen and transfer enrollments in our two largest units, LS&A and Engineering, with less attention devoted to the six other units that also admit freshmen directly. Graduate enrollment planning has been largely nonexistent outside the professional schools.

We have begun an effort to improve our planning process. A key element is the development of a system that places responsibilities for enrollment and revenue decisions on the deans. This is a radical change for Michigan, and we have a long way to go. However, the PACE reports have clearly set the stage for such an effort; and the deans, many of whom have had great difficulty in planning for wide swings in enrollment, seem eager to undertake the challenge. The process opened with meetings with admissions officers and key associate deans from LS&A and Engineering. Discussions focused on historical data on applications, admissions, and yields provided by our office of academic planning and analysis. The graduate school also participates in these discussions because no unit can deal independently with undergraduate and graduate enrollment. These discussions will then go to the departmental levels, where the greatest uncontrolled variations in graduate enrollment have occurred.

Within two years we hope to have enrollment plans in place for schools and colleges at the undergraduate level and for departments at the graduate level. Deans currently need program details as well as the overall enrollment mix to plan scheduling and staffing. Because we do not control positions centrally, such decisions reside at the school and college level. Position control at the provost level would be a very radical change for Michigan, and there is no need for it if we can achieve the goal of giving the deans responsibility for revenue as well as expenditure.

Annual Budget Actions

During our last fiscal year the university's state appropriation was reduced by one percent, a rollback of about $2.6 million, which in turn reduced our overall general fund by slightly under half a percent. We decided to reduce our base budgets by an equivalent amount and asked each of the vice presidents to cut about 0.45 percent from their budgets. How they chose to implement this was their decision. We simply asked for account numbers and reduced the appropriations as indicated.

About $2 million of the total reduction came from academic units. We exempted financial aid and certain mandatory expenditures and then applied the cuts to the academic units quite differently, ranging from 0.12 percent to about 0.8 percent. These cuts were not formula driven but were based on enrollment data, quality perceptions, and the relative subsidies indicated by the PACE model. Major complaints were received from only two units. The one with the largest percentage cut and the one with the smallest, both saying it was too much.

For the current budget we followed past practices, with some modest exceptions. Each vice president was given the same percentage allocation after certain mandatory expenditures for debt service, utilities, and financial aid. An additional one percent was taken off the top for reallocation to the academic units by the provost. In general, vice presidential areas were increased three percent, but units were asked to attempt salary programs of four percent or better, thus forcing unit reallocations of about one percent. The overall one percent taken off the top was allocated to several areas: a special allocation to the library to deal with very rapid escalation in serial costs, a special program to add minority faculty, a special addition to our financial aid budgets, and an additional $2.2 million designated for meeting critical academic needs.

These funds for critical academic needs were allocated differentially to the schools and colleges in nearly the same but opposite patterns as the cuts made in the last fiscal year. The net result of cuts and differential allocations has been a reallocation of relative budgets of well over one percent to the schools and colleges. Again, the total magnitude is not great, but the direction is on target.

Space Costs

Currently, all costs associated with space use by our general fund units are borne centrally. Space is thus a free good to most units, and not unexpectedly it is viewed as such. This means that classrooms are used heavily in the middle of the day and hardly used in early mornings or late afternoons, and we are seen as having a classroom shortage. Laboratories for faculty use are in very short supply even though some may not have been used very actively for some time. Who wants to move someone out if it doesn't cost anything to keep the space?

We are beginning an effort to charge units for space. Inevitably such a change will influence the vigor with which units protest to central services for maintenance, and we anticipate asking other institutions for advice on handling this culture change.

Our chances of another negative supplemental appropriation from the state are high, and uncertainty over indirect cost recovery has caused us considerable concern about our current year revenue estimates. An educated guess suggests that reductions might be around $12 million, or roughly two percent of this year's general fund budget. No one wants to plan for such a possibility, but the threat is real. Vice presidents have been asked to plan for such cuts and to build that flexibility into this year's expenditures as well as their plans for the future. Deans have been asked to do the same thing. How well they have done remains to be assessed.

Total Quality Management Effort

Changing our management style to one of total quality management was a major recommendation of the costs task force. The process of change has barely begun, but many of us already believe that it is essential to our future.

We are fortunate that the university hospital has been engaged in a total quality management effort for about four years. We have the opportunity to learn from its experiences and to enlist the expertise of key staff. The hospital is firmly committed to the effort, which has not only improved the quality of much of its activity but has also been cost effective, demonstrating dollar savings, for example, on the order of $14 million for an expenditure of some $2.5 million. There are many nonquantifiable improvements, too, in patient satisfaction and employee satisfaction, as well as measurable improvements in quality. The increasing involvement of physicians in the process is especially encouraging because it suggests that we can anticipate faculty involvement after several years of demonstrated success in service activities.

Several academic units within the university, among them the accounts payable office, the information technology division, and the entire engineering college, have also begun total quality management efforts, and all are encouraged by the efforts to date.

Against this background we held an executive management quality retreat in August 1991, with participation by most senior university officers, several key deans, and about six or eight key senior staff members. The retreat was facilitated by a consulting firm that the hospital had utilized that is now working with the university and featured basic introductions to total quality management, team- and consensus-building exercises, and the development of a draft mission and vision statement for the university.

Next steps included the appointment of a Quality Council by the president and the council's ratification of the selection of a design team. The council is concerned with overall policy and resource allocation issues. It is chaired by the president and includes all of the university officers, several deans, and a couple of key senior staff. Among its more significant assignments are to write the next draft of the mission and vision statements and to approve the output of the design team's efforts. The major product expected from the design team is the implementation plan for our university quality program.

The design team is composed of sixteen individuals representing major university areas, among them the associate vice president for academic affairs, the associate vice president for business operations, the associate dean for LS&A budgets, the dean of the university library, the director of academic planning and analysis, the assistant vice president for admissions and financial aid, several faculty, and other key staff. Though still in the early stages of training and deliberations, the team has developed a good feeling of group effort.

Much remains to be done. We don't have a very clear planning effort, but we hope the wide variety of strategic and tactical activities discussed here will lead to the development of a planning process. If we can accomplish this without unduly disturbing the flexibility that is critical to maintaining and improving our reputation as an innovative research university, we will have exceeded our expectations.

DRAFT MISSION AND VISION STATEMENTS
UNIVERSITY OF MICHIGAN
EXECUTIVE MANAGEMENT M-QUALITY WORKSHOP

Mission Statement

To serve the people of Michigan and the world through preeminence in creating, communicating, preserving, and applying knowledge and academic values, and in developing leaders and citizens who challenge the present and enrich the future.

Vision Statement

- To be a source of pride for the people of Michigan.
- To have a place in the dreams of every potential student and faculty member.
- To have a place in the heart of every member of the university community.
- To have an international image as a community that honors human diversity—and a reality to match the image.
- To be a community of scholars in which ideas are challenged but people are welcomed and nurtured.
- To be the employer of choice.
- To be a campus that is an ideal learning environment for faculty, students, and staff; an ideal workplace for nonteaching staff; and a campus in which the responsibility of staff for creating that environment is recognized and valued.

Chapter 5 ─────────────────────────

The Stanford Experience I: The Administrative Process

Susan M. Schaffer
Vice President, Administrative Resources
Stanford University

Major structural changes need to take place on the administrative side at Stanford, as at other universities, in order to support the major reductions we have already made and will continue to make in our operating budget. There are appropriate, applicable practices in the corporate world; and as this is an area where I spent nineteen years in major staff and line vice president positions, I have a particular perspective to offer.

In the decades of the 1970s and 1980s the environment changed from one of unrestricted growth to severe recession. During that recession, I headed a corporate division of 9,000 service employees, and it was my responsibility to significantly reduce my overhead and to rework the service we provided so that we could continue to satisfy our customers while cutting costs to the greatest extent possible. The outcomes of that mandate were:

- a reduction of the management work force by 50 percent,
- a way to micromanage the allocation of employees to match specific customer volumes,
- the creation of employee resource and support systems that were both market-competitive and market-specific.

In other words, we turned things upside down—while continuing to focus on the mission of our organization—and wound up with an organization that was so directly on target for the competitive times that it remained in place, intact, for eight years, quite an unusual feat in corporate America.

To my mind, Stanford and other universities and colleges with which I have had opportunities to compare notes are in an exactly similar position to that of corporate America in the early 1980s. Our world has been turned on its ear. Revenues are trending the wrong way, expenses threaten to surge the moment we take our eye off budget controls, and our public images have been tarnished through constant governmental and media scrutiny. To choose to believe that this is a short-term phenomenon that will pass is to postulate that colleges and universities are outside the rest of the universe. We are in for a long, difficult, undernourished time, which is why it is interesting to review the changing work at Stanford in the context of its relation to our budget cuts.

REVIEWING ORGANIZATIONAL EFFECTIVENESS

As a preliminary to our budget efforts, we reviewed ways of improving our organizational effectiveness. There was a grass-roots sentiment that something was wrong; the process was endless, sluggish, and in some cases sorely out of date. People felt it throughout the university. So we launched several efforts to pinpoint what needed changing. Among them were:

- a review of human resources that asked the question "Who's in charge?"
- a review of student services that asked whether its myriad reporting relationships should be brought together under one leader.
- an experiment to bring a new payroll system on-line that would not have endless permutations built in to satisfy each department on campus.

We had no specific expectations in terms of dollar savings, but we were looking for improvement. Within months of the startup of these projects, however, we realized that we had a mounting budget problem, so we added dollar expectations to the projects.

The model of this process gave us the idea that during budget cuts we could also improve work effectiveness—as a matter of fact, we knew that if we didn't do so, we would greatly disappoint many of our staff. Work effectiveness, therefore, became one of our explicit goals during budget repositioning and remains an explicit goal for our current process of budget reduction. With a few notable exceptions, however, we are not changing the work.

The Reasons Why

First, Stanford's administrative side, like that of many universities, has grown without plan, without management systems, and without the principles and infrastructure necessary to meet the challenges of the 1990s.

Second, we have not clearly defined, supported, and reinforced a strong administrative and leadership culture that is different from the faculty culture. Tangible signs of trouble include the lack of clear accountability, the fact of minimal strategic planning, the absence of measurement systems, large numbers of service complaints, and a very muddled process of handling them. During our high-growth times this weakness in management infrastructure was invisible, but our current budget crises are bringing these inadequacies to light. Our changing times require changed expectations for effective management.

Some people might be alarmed at the notion of creating a separate culture for those administrative staffs that do not reside in a school, the area that we dub academic administration. This is a time when we are trying to reduce the tension and the consequent gulf between faculty and administration. Should we be talking about building two camps when we need to come together around our joint crisis?

But there are signs that we are ready for two camps. There is recognition that a spillover of faculty characteristics to administration may not, after all, be a good idea. For example, bringing open-ended inquiry and the search for truth over to the administrative side may get translated into looking for 100-percent solutions. Having a very deep expertise in a narrow field can translate into a manager who is technically competent but lacks the perspective and people skills needed to build a functional organization. There is also considerable sentiment from the administrative staff that they need a separate identity and validation of their contribution to the mission of the university. And there is even a shift among faculty at Stanford from being critiques of administration to being consumers of its services. This became particularly apparent in the recent budget process when faculty had an opportunity to question and observe more closely what administration does.

A NEW ADMINISTRATIVE STRUCTURE

Given the need for a new administrative infrastructure and some apparent readiness for it, Stanford has proposed a new solution. We believe that adapting the corporate bottom-line model to university requirements has potential for focusing the efforts of the administration, providing support to both faculty and the mission of the university and establishing the rationale for creating a new administrative structure. It is the bottom line, after all, that drives most behavior in the corporate world. People all through a company understand it and also understand that their actions are supposed to influence it. The closer one's position is to affecting the bottom line, the more the individual feels a stake in the enterprise. For the college and university world, we propose turning the model upside down.

Establishing a "Top Line"

Consider that all efforts in higher education ought to be in support of the academic and research missions of the university. Those missions are lofty, intangible goals—something to reach for and nourish. The administration's achievements in support of that mission represent an upward contribution to what we'll call "the top line."

Here is a scenario in which the academic faculty and their leaders are "the academy" and the members of the administrative staff "the administration."

As the academic year is closing, a set of meetings takes place between the academy and the administration to set goals for the year ahead. The idea is that the administration will adopt specific objectives that, once achieved, will support the university's teaching and research mission and also strengthen the academy. The objectives could take several forms: to return budget savings to pools for academic innovation, to improve services, or to resolve specific problems. The various objectives are assigned to administrative units along with clear accountability and expectations of specific results. They are published, along with dates by which their completion is expected. At the end of the year the administration reports on its results, receives comments from the academy and its peers, and embarks on another set of objectives for the next year.

The notion of administration collaborating with faculty to establish goals and objectives would seem highly likely to get the concurrence of Stanford faculty. Why wouldn't they be prepared to think of the academy as the top line and the administration as existing to contribute to it? As with most management concepts, however, the difficulty is not in the concept but in the doing. To have the top-line concept become reality, there have to be some administrative building blocks in place—the administrative infrastructure, in fact. To be effective that infrastructure must include the following:

1. a strategic plan
2. organizational focus

3. measurement systems
4. individual objectives and evaluations systems
5. communication channels
6. a well-defined administrative culture

The Strategic Plan

The university must develop a strategic plan, which includes a statement of its mission that is specific enough to provide guidance for new programs. It includes an analysis of the economic, cultural, social, political, and competitive environment. It also includes a set of goals for achieving the mission in light of these environmental considerations and a declaration of strategies and tactics appropriate for pursuing the goals. The more dialogue with the academy this plan includes, the better. Such a clear and specific statement forms an umbrella under which faculty and administrators should and can see their common purpose and mission. Lacking it, anybody can wish for, demand, or resist anything. Without a strategic plan the administration offers itself up again and again for criticism and dismemberment. If we do not set forth the context and focus of our actions, we cannot expect the faculty to be supportive, much less grateful.

Organizational Focus and Clarity

The strategic plan then drives the next step, the organizational focus and clarity that bring the plan down to the individual unit level. Each unit is asked to determine its unique mission, its value, the products and services it delivers, and the consumers of those services. In other words, organizational focus and clarity works by ensuring that each organizational unit fits tightly into the purpose of the institution. Unless each unit knows its exact role within the university and can focus its products and services toward that role, it will frustrate all attempts to provide top-line support. In fact, units that lack such clarity will only create organizational "noise" that distracts from the top line. In these budget-cutting times this process can also be called work restructuring or reengineering.

Measurement Systems

Organizational focus and clarity will ultimately drive this next step. We have made some progress at Stanford in laying out benchmark performance indicators that, at a glance, can give a reading on the health and performance of an administrative unit. Such indicators can include unit cost, productivity, service-quality survey feedback, budget performance, requisition or work-order turn time, sick leave data, and affirmative action opportunity and results, to name just a few. Without agreed upon methods of measuring a unit's performance there is no way to move effectively toward a results orientation because there will always be debate about the validity of what is being measured.

A top line demands measurement systems. Without measurement any system of declaring objectives is open to misinterpretation, and it is all too easy to set the wrong objective. At Stanford there is great resistance to measurement, particularly from the schools. This is an issue of autonomy and control, and the resistance stems from lack of positive experience. If measurement is to happen anywhere, it must start in the central administration. In the long run it is bound to strengthen and sharpen us.

Individual Measurement Systems

Once a strategic plan, organizational focus, and performance measures are in place, a top-line orientation requires that the administration establish staff objectives and performance measurement systems for individuals. There is a tendency we all share to evaluate staff on the basis of their relationships, especially their relationships with those above them. But that is not a sufficient basis for evaluation. We need to set objectives with individual staff members—objectives that are measurable, that drive results which enhance and support the department's mission. Evaluation solely by presentation is unfair; and ultimately, without specific measures and data to acknowledge success, staff tend to retreat and take very few risks.

An evaluation system that requires results as well as a display of management skills is at the heart of structural change in university management. Unless individuals are held accountable for achieving a set of clear-cut objectives, there is no way for the institution to drive results to a top line. You simply cannot wish your way toward goal achievement.

Communication Channels

It may be the autonomous nature of the university that has prevented formation of formal, face-to-face communication channels. Or it may be the existence of a university press that passes on the word in traditional ways. But to carry us through the 1990s and to get staff on board with the top line, we must create formal and frequent occasions for them to understand the mission, focus, issues, and opportunities that face their units, the administration, and the university as a whole. We must also expect and encourage informal management styles by walking around and by seeking employee involvement in identifying problems and finding solutions for them. Autonomy is a faculty domain, not an administrative one. We need to get staff pulling together toward specific accomplishments that benefit the institution, and doing so will not be possible without a very specific communication effort.

We have made progress at Stanford—vice presidents now meet more frequently with staff. But without constant reminders from leadership, this tends to falter. There is also a need to work communication down through the organization, so that each leader throughout the hierarchy understands that this is part of his or her job. The resistance to this type of communication process is remarkable—and it directly reflects the importance of fitting the next, and final, piece of this structural puzzle into place.

A Well-Defined Administrative Culture

The last management requirement for our being able to implement a top-line concept at Stanford is that we actively define what an administrative culture consists of. In a time of change it is critical that leadership pays conscious attention both to the culture that exists and to the one that is needed. The staff will be demoralized—and indeed some of our staff currently are almost paralyzed. They have never gone through such wide-ranging layoffs and organizational change; they have never experienced the tarnishing of the image of higher education. They feel that their personal reputations have been impugned as a result of the bashing Stanford has received in the media. The staff need to feel grounded, to hear the values affirmed that we continue to hold dear; but they also need urging to actively accept the ideas, values, and principles that are appropriate to our new times. Because at Stanford the institution is so autonomous, there has not been a culture that defined such areas as ethical behavior, the treatment of employees, the difference between being faculty and being staff, attitudes toward union agreements, the right to set expectations for staff or how to treat nonperformers.

Who is accountable for fixing employee problems? How much staff involvement and participation do we want? How important is accountability? How will we assign it and get it? What are the rules for getting agreement in administration? What are the rules for how to act if one disagrees?

Such questions float like fall leaves an a slow moving stream, bumping into one another, overlapping at times, but never amounting to much until they get dammed up around some obstacle. Our highly intelligent staffs are crying out for discourse and clarity because they know that when common understandings exist, they spend less time in frustration and more in action. Defining the role of the staff in the complex environment of the university makes it possible for them to feel grounded, to have the confidence that can empower their actions.

THE IMPLICATIONS

So the simple idea of a top-line orientation turns out to have extraordinary implications because one really cannot get there from here without having to tend to the essential structural issues of strategic plans, organizational focus, measurement systems, individual objectives and performance systems, communication channels, and the definition of administrative culture. I believe that for Stanford, and for many other institutions, these fundamental changes will in fact separate faculty and administration while, at the same time, strengthening their relationships. For the first time, administrators will be able to clearly show what they are accomplishing in ways that the academy can either accept or reject. It may be too much to expect appreciation, but I guarantee that the impact internally on administrative staff will be an elevated sense of self, pride in accomplishment, a buckling down to correct obvious and declared problems, and a vast improvement in administrative functioning and budget control.

At Stanford we are poised to make significant financial changes; yet we are fearful that unless we make administrative changes too, we will not be able to hold our new financial course. We can see the type of administrative structural changes that can ballast our financial future, but those changes are so vast and deep that we may after all lack the courage to make them. We are in the midst of academic leadership change, but who will be responsible for leading administrative change?

In the past two years we have gone through more organizational recalibration than we ever imagined possible, and we are seeing more and more clearly what must be done next. So as we take $43 million out of the budget in the next years, we will also be gathering our strength for the administrative changes that are essential for the ultimate health of our institution.

Chapter 6

The Stanford Experience II: The Financial Process

Timothy R. Warner

*Associate Vice President and
Director of University Budgets
Stanford University*

At the time of the 1991 Stanford Forum for Higher Education Futures, the university was engaged in its third program in as many years aimed at achieving budget reduction and organizational change. This time the effort was to reduce $43 million from its $365 million operating budget. By the time this program is completed in 1993–94, Stanford will have made budget adjustments (expense reductions and income enhancements) of $66 million (in 1993–94 dollars) over this period.

The purpose of this report is to provide a chronological and thematic overview of the budget-adjustment processes in which Stanford has been engaged since 1989. In some sense this is a progress report, as much remains to be done. However, a considerable amount has already been accomplished—at times under the trying uncertainties of the all too well publicized indirect cost controversy. Despite the turmoil of those events, the Stanford community is clearly pulling together to correct the serious budget imbalance and to continue its tradition of excellence in teaching and research.

For purposes of organization and convenience, I have divided the budget adjustment efforts of the past several years into four chronologic periods.

For the purposes of this report, the School of Medicine, which has about a $60 million operating budget, is excluded. The school operates on a formula arrangement with the university and is well into its own budget-reduction exercise—a topic for another day.

However, it is most important to note that these four efforts do not represent an approach that was planned at the outset as an integrated, phased effort of budget reduction and organizational change. Rather, at the start of each such "effort" there was absolutely no expectation that a subsequent episode would follow. Unfortunately, as the last several years have unfolded, external events affecting Stanford have clearly moved faster than our ability to respond, and subsequent efforts have proven to be essential. The four phases have been as follows:

- Effort 1—Begun in summer 1989, this effort was called "Action Plans for Change." It represented an attempt to simplify and streamline the university's organizational structure and decision-making processes.
- Effort 2—Begun in February 1990, this program was called "Repositioning" and was aimed at reducing administrative expense by $22 million, or 13 percent of the applicable budget base. Only administrative and support functions were affected in the Repositioning program.
- Effort 3—Begun in mid-1990, this phase focused on a reorganization of the university's central administrative structure.
- Effort 4—Begun in spring 1991, the objective of this phase is to make budget adjustments of $43 million. Unlike Repositioning, both academic and nonacademic budgets will be subject to reduction, and there will be efforts to increase some sources of revenue.

BACKGROUND

The story of Stanford's budget adjustment efforts really begins with the legacy of the 1980s. That period was one of strong growth for Stanford and for other private research universities. The following average annual growth rates at Stanford from 1980–1988 give a general idea of the magnitude of the expansion that occurred: real budget growth of 6.7 percent; real sponsored research growth of 5.6 percent; real growth in gifts of 10 percent. Infrastructure grew considerably as well during this period, as reflected in a 28 percent growth in staff, while the faculty grew at just 5 percent over the eight-year period.

As this growth boomed along there was little reason to believe that it wouldn't continue. Stanford was well into the largest fund-raising campaign in the history of higher education, significant growth in facilities construction was projected, and the faculty appointments process was producing excellent results. But in the midst of all this optimism, there were emerging signs of concern. Some of the more notable signals were:

- Small budget deficits were recorded for 1988 and 1989, and the trustees reluctantly approved the first planned deficit budget in fifteen years for 1989–90.
- The indirect cost rate was projected to increase into the low 80 percent range, due principally to facilities construction and infrastructure costs.
- There was growing frustration with decision-making processes and service delivery throughout the university. Both faculty and staff began to complain about the seemingly endless review processes required for even the most simple administrative tasks, the price of internally provided services, and the strong reliance on consensus-based decision-making processes.
- External criticism of tuition increases had been growing throughout the '80s.

Although the future certainly looked bright in the late '80s, the boom essentially ended in about 1988 as some of these issues began to express themselves negatively in financial terms. At the time, only a small group of trustees and administrators recognized that a period of contraction was likely. However, the magnitude of the changes Stanford has gone through since then could not have been predicted by anyone.

EFFORT 1—ACTION PLANS FOR CHANGE

With the approval of a $2 million planned deficit budget for 1989–90, the trustees established an informal committee (the Ad Hoc Committee on Financial Strategy) to work with Provost James N. Rosse in developing a set of strategic planning directions. One of the first outcomes of that interaction was the creation of an effort called "Action Plans for Change" (APC). This group, whose steering committee included the provost, a dean, and several vice presidents, was focused on providing alternatives for structural and process change.

One of the galvanizing events of that group's early work was a visit to the Union Pacific Railroad, run by Stanford trustee Michael H. Walsh, who was also a member of the Ad Hoc Committee. Walsh had spent the previous three years reducing cost and increasing productivity at the railroad and had met with great success. (Stanford's experiences with UP are chronicled in the November/December 1990 issue of *Change*, in an article titled "Stanford and the Railroad.") While the lessons in for-profit cost reduction cannot necessarily be applied on an item for item basis in a university setting, it was clear that higher education had a good deal to learn from the corporate streamlining experience in which so many companies engaged in the 1980s.

Perhaps the most immediate result of the APC interaction with Union Pacific was the creation of a series of "action teams" to understand and make recommendations for change in a number of problem areas and processes. UP had done well with this technique, and it seemed to hold promise for Stanford.

Identifying the problem areas, however required some listening on the part of the APC steering committee. The committee conducted over 100 interviews with faculty, staff, and administrators. Out of those discussions came four working principles that would guide the efforts of the group. In addition, the conversations helped the group identify a small set of problem areas on which to focus. The operating principles for APC focused on simplifying the university's organizations, processes, and decision-making enterprise. They were:

- simplify organizational structures
- simplify processes
- develop stronger client/provider relationships
- change the management culture to make the first three principles work

Guided by these principles, action teams were established in the following areas to review the current situation and to make recommendations: student services, human resources management, facilities planning, libraries, and the reporting structure under the provost.

The teams were launched in the fall of 1989 with the goal of providing recommendations within six months. But as would happen several times over the succeeding two years, external events overtook the effort put in place. In the case of the APC effort, just two months after it began the Loma Prieta earthquake struck, causing $150 million in damage to the Stanford campus. If the development of a recovery plan for that event wasn't enough to keep the university engaged, then in January revised budget projections showed a major income shortfall due to a drop in the projected growth rate of government-sponsored research. As a result of these two events, it appeared that Stanford would need to move beyond the APC effort into a program that combined the efforts for structural and process change with some more highly focused budget reductions.

EFFORT 2—REPOSITIONING

Although a number of other research universities were beginning to feel the pressure to slow the growth rate of their budgets from the halcyon days of the '80s, none was moving as aggressively as Stanford was about to in the winter of 1990. When the university became convinced that it needed to take a significant budget reduction in order to produce balanced budgets for some years to come, a program called "Repositioning" was announced in February 1990. The Repositioning program had four objectives:

1. to contain growth in key income items, most significantly by pledging to hold tuition growth to inflation plus one percent
2. to reduce administrative expenses in the operating budget by $22 million, or 12 percent
3. to expand the APC efforts of process and structural reform
4. to constrain the growth of Stanford's highly ambitious building program

Although Repositioning moved beyond APC with the budget-reduction component, it was meant to be more than a budget-cutting exercise. It was clear to all involved that Stanford needed to change its management culture and restructure some of its principal operations in order to sustain any of the expense reductions.

The Repositioning Planning Process

In comparison to many university budget-reduction processes, Repositioning had some rather unusual characteristics.

Top-down process. Repositioning was very much a top-down process. A steering committee, chaired by the provost, made up of three senior faculty, key operating vice presidents, a trustee, and an executive of a major local company, ran the process. The consultation in which this group chose to engage was highly focused and was concluded in a matter of weeks. A broad-scale consensus-building process was not deemed necessary to move the process forward.

Differential reduction targets. Budget-reduction targets ranging from 5 percent to 30 percent were developed by the steering committee, reflecting the widely held belief that across-the-board administrative cuts would not be in the university's best interests.

Use of liaison teams. The steering committee divided itself into "liaison teams" of three or four to work with each of the units in developing budget-reduction strategies. This would prove to be a most useful way to operate in order to assess the impacts of various reductions across units.

Communication an essential ingredient. The committee took a cue from the Union Pacific experience and placed heavy emphasis on communicating the key features of the process and the motivation behind it. The communication process was meant to be two way, with frequent opportunities for local units—and individuals—to provide feedback into the process.

Repositioning—Results

When the Repositioning planning process was completed in June, 1990, we had identified the full $22 million in budget cuts and were projecting modest surpluses in the subsequent three years as a result of the implementation of the reductions. At the time it looked like a considerable success, with some of the following outcomes:

- Most of the APC action teams had completed their recommendations. Among the most notable: the human resources team, which endorsed a 30 percent cut in that function across the university; the student services team, which recommended the consolidation of a number of student service units under one leadership; and the libraries team, which recommended the merger of the libraries and information resources.
- All units had developed plans for achieving reductions. The reductions were to occur principally through elimination of some functions, heavy reliance on consolidation of activities, and reduction of support roles in many areas of the administration.
- Frequent communication by the provost and the steering committee to the affected units and to the community at large was an important outcome. This emphasis on communication would put the institution in a good position to address future budget-related issues.

But for the full effects of the Repositioning effort to be felt, considerable additional work needed to be done over the longer term. The lasting benefits of such a program were in reorganization, work restructuring, and reengineering. These kinds of changes could not be accomplished overnight. In fact, it was not entirely clear that Stanford—or any of its sister institutions—had the knowledge of how to restructure and reengineer work in a way that would provide significant and lasting expense reduction. Nor was it clear that the consensus base decision making would be changed. These kinds of complex and difficult issues would take at least two to three years to work through.

As the Repositioning planning process concluded in mid-1990, it seemed that there would be time for such fundamental changes to be explored. However, external events once again overwhelmed Stanford's best laid plans and set the stage for yet another—and this time much more significant—budget-reduction exercise. Before providing a progress report on those efforts, however, we will briefly review an important interim stage—a reorganization of the central administration, which would prove to be an essential element in the subsequent budget-adjustment process.

EFFORT 3—REORGANIZATION

The principal focus of the reorganization was threefold:

- to elevate the leadership and management of the schools to the highest priority and to rely on the deans for policy guidance much more extensively than had been the case in the past
- to strengthen the connections between the schools and the support units through the development of the School Management Group (SMG). The purpose of the SMG was to bring together the administrative deans of Stanford's seven schools and the principal service-providing organizations in a regular and systematic way to address the constant flow of issues
- to simplify the administrative organization of the university through the clear delineation of responsibilities to the vice presidents

These changes had a number of important results. Perhaps the most important was that the University Cabinet (in the persons of the president, the provost, and the deans) began to take collective responsibility for the policy direction of the institution and for general university management. While the deans had obviously played important leadership roles in the past, it had been the Administrative Council, made up of the president, provost, and vice presidents, to which the majority of important university policy issues were directed. As it turned out, the creation of the University Cabinet occurred just in the nick of time. With the deans fully and appropriately engaged, the cabinet would play a critical role in shaping and directing the subsequent budget-adjustment process.

Two other significant outcomes resulted from the reorganization:

- A number of student service units, which heretofore had reported to the provost and other vice presidents, were consolidated into a single VP area.

- The libraries and the information technology functions were merged into a single vice presidency (called "Libraries and Information Resources") as a way of positioning the institution to take advantage of the emerging synergies between the traditional library functions and information technologies.

The reorganization was indeed a timely accomplishment as it clarified policy roles and strengthened lines of accountability and responsibility.

EFFORT 4—THE CURRENT STRATEGIC PLANNING AND BUDGETING PROCESS

The controversy over Stanford's relationship with the federal government on indirect costs issues has been chronicled in the media in some detail, although with questionable levels of accuracy. It is not the purpose of this presentation to describe the events or points of view of that controversy—or to correct the many inaccuracies that had been reported. Our focus, instead, will be on the indirect cost controversy as one—but not the only—contributor to the budget problem that we're now in the midst of addressing.

As we speak, the university needs to make adjustments in its operating budget (exclusive of the Medical School) of approximately $43 million (or 12 percent). This program is designed to be implemented over two years, 1992–93 and 1993–94, at which time we are projected to reach a balanced position. To provide a transition for planning and implementation and to address the accumulated deficits of 1990–91 and 1991–92, the trustees authorized the use of $100 million of reserves.

In May 1991 a process was developed to identifying the magnitude of the problem and to provide plans for budget adjustments. Some of the key features of the process to date follow.

Universitywide Participation

Many constituencies actively participated in the budget-adjustment and strategic planning effort. It has involved hundreds of people from across the university spectrum engaged in thousands of hours of information gathering, analysis, discussion, and decision making.

The various committees and their leadership began the process with the understanding that such an effort touches all members of the Stanford community, and they committed themselves to making the process both understandable and accessible. In order to ensure this climate of openness, faculty, staff, students, and alumni were kept informed in a variety of ways throughout the entire process (see section on communications below).

Cabinet Committee on Budget and Strategic Planning (CC-BSP). Leading the effort has been the CC-BSP, which reported to the University Cabinet and was given primary responsibility for developing and implementing an overall budget-reduction program and strategic planning effort for Stanford. The charge to the CC-BSP was as follows:

> The first task of the CC-BSP will be to develop proposals for consideration by the University Cabinet designed to change the scope and priorities of the University to fit developing budget realities. The Committee will also oversee implementation of the proposals it develops as they receive Cabinet approval . . . . The budget for 1992–93 will be substantially reduced compared to the current year. The reduction will need to be accomplished on a permanent basis that will oblige restructuring academic priorities and reorganization of academic and supporting units.

The CC-BSP was chaired by the provost and included representation from across the university, including faculty and students. The group met regularly, developing and reviewing proposals—unit by unit—as well as for their institutional impact. The CC-BSP's work was done in coordination with the University Cabinet, the Senate Committee on Education and Scholarship at Stanford (SC-BSS), the Trustee Sub-Committee on Budget and Strategic Planning, and the many faculty, students, and staff who provided input.

The Senate Committee on Education and Scholarship at Stanford (SC-ESS). Formed by the Academic Senate, the SC-ESS was charged to lead a comprehensive study of the research and educational goals that should guide the processes of reform and renewal of the university during a period when Stanford is obliged to reduce its operating budget by approximately 15 percent.

SC-ESS also examined all aspects of the structure, procedures, and policies that were essential for guaranteeing the strength of Stanford as a leading institution for education, scholarship, and research. As an instrument of the Senate and, ultimately, the Academic Council, the SC-ESS brought its findings and recommendations to the Senate through that body's Steering Committee. The committee acted in an advisory capacity only and worked closely with the CC-BSP. SC-ESS was aided in its work by task forces that studied administrative services, graduate and professional education, research and scholarship, revenue enhancement, and undergraduate education. More than 50 faculty members contributed to the intense effort.

In a set of 18 preliminary recommendations, the SC-ESS noted its strong support for the university libraries, proposed creation of an endowment to protect nonsponsored scholarship in the humanities, suggested ideas on income enhancement, and proposed changes in the structure of financial decision making at the university.

Liaison Teams. The liaison teams were internal working groups that were formed by the CC-BSP to help guide the planning process in the local units. The teams worked directly and regularly with the deans and vice presidents, listening to plans, offering advice, analyzing proposals, and making recommendations directly to the CC-BSP. The teams, which included faculty, administrators, and students, were formed from the membership of the CC-BSP and the SC-ESS, additional students, chairs of the Academic Council committees, and others. The liaison teams were a key element to the success of the process.

The Trustee Sub-Committee on Budget and Strategic Planning. The Trustee Sub-Committee on Budget and Strategic Planning was formed by the Board of Trustees from its local membership to provide a means for monitoring the planning process. The committee continues to meet on most Saturdays to review progress and provide step-by-step feedback during the entire budget and strategic planning process. They have consulted widely with faculty.

Local Committees. Many different forms of consultation were employed by the schools and support units in developing plans to meet budget reduction targets. Deans, vice presidents, and directors of major support units created ad hoc committees and task forces representative of their constituencies. The idea behind this structure was to have programs and services reviewed and plans formed by the people closest to them. Hundreds of employees participated in this grass-roots effort.

CC-BSP Task Forces. Several task forces were formed in the early stages of the budget-planning effort, drawing their membership from the Cabinet, the CC-BSP, the SC-ESS, internal experts, and others. The principal CC-BSP task forces were:

- Task Force on Organizational Decentralization—charged with investigating the consequences of adopting a more decentralized structure of decision making and function at Stanford
- Task Force on Costs and Income—charged with examining the principal sources of revenue and uses of that revenue, by school and activ-

ity, "attributing" expense and revenue to units where possible

- Task Force on Early Retirement Incentive—charged with designing possible early retirement incentive programs for faculty and staff

Timeline and Activities

April-June 1991. The CC-BSP and SC-ESS were formed, and the budget-reduction and strategic planning process was launched. At the June board meeting an initial estimate of a $43-million budget problem in the nonformula areas of the university was presented. The board endorsed a planning process to balance the operating budgets by 1993–94 and the necessary use of reserves through 1993–94. It also suggested budget actions to reduce shortfalls in fiscal years 1991 and 1992. During the spring the Stanford community was informed of the timetable and planning process for the overall effort.

July-October 1991. The target-setting process began in July, when the CC-BSP developed initial ranges of potential budget adjustments for each unit to consider. Specifically, schools were given a range of 7 percent–13 percent and support units 15 percent–21 percent. Two initial planning efforts then followed. On August 15 each unit developed a written document outlining mission, comparative data, and other information. In a second report, completed on September 5, each unit provided detailed scenarios of the kinds of program and service reductions they would envision at various levels of budget cuts and specified the consequences of those actions. This information was reviewed extensively by the cabinet, the CC-BSP, SC-ESS and the liaison teams.

During this phase the president and provost released their vision statement, which would come to guide the process, entitled "Stanford beyond the Watershed." SC-ESS also developed a "Goals and Guidelines " document, and its task force presented recommendations. It is also important to note that two faculty open forums were held to discuss SC-ESS recommendations, and several town meetings were held for faculty and staff to provide input. Additional work was done on resizing the budget problem, and in conjunction with the review of the preliminary plans the $43-million target was established. In mid-October the president and provost, with the full endorsement of the cabinet, made decisions on specific budget reduction targets for each unit, which were then announced to the community on October 22.

October-December 1991. During this period schools and administrative areas began developing plans for implementing budget targets in local units. This work was done in consultation with local advisory groups and the liaison teams.

January-March 1992. Plans for budget adjustments from individual units were to be submitted on January 17 and reviewed by the CC-BSP and the cabinet. They were also to be reviewed for consistency with one another and with overall university goals and priorities.

April-June 1992. Schools and administrative areas developed detailed implementation plans for carrying out their budget adjustments. The plans affect their budget base beginning with the 1992–93 fiscal year and will be concluded in the 1993–94 fiscal year.

Communications

A broad-based communications strategy has been underway since the start of the process to build awareness within the community of the goals, objectives, sections, and desired outcome of the budget-planning effort. Information, provided in a clear, straightforward, and timely manner, was tailored to answer key questions. Those included, but were not limited to, identifying the decision makers, the status of the process, the direction in which Stanford was headed, how faculty, staff, and students could get involved, and the values and principles guiding the process.

A variety of vehicles was used to keep people informed. Prime among them was use of campus periodicals—the *Campus Report, Stanford Observer,* and the *Stanford Daily.* A series of letters from the president and provost, a number of town meetings, Faculty Senate meetings, and Stanford alumni gatherings provided additional venues to discuss budget and strategic planning progress. Students were kept informed via Student Senate briefings, meetings in the residences, and a special town meeting. The CC-BSP also met with various groups representing the campus minority communities.

CURRENT ISSUES

The following issues emerge from our current efforts.

The Strategy Question

What is emerging from this process, based on the preliminary plans put forward, is a Stanford whose basic outlines and landscape will not change a great deal. There will be consolidation of administrative units, reductions in some teaching staff, more students on the campus at the graduate (master's) level, and additional squeezing of income sources at the margin. Service levels on the support side of the institution will be reduced, and there will be a few functions we will do without. But once this process is complete, there will still be seven strong schools in the university, a dynamic undergraduate program, and a very clear emphasis on research and support for research.

These kinds of likely results are entirely appropriate but would not necessarily have been predicted at the start of the process. Many on campus have been predicting a more significant restructuring. Indeed, there will be concern that the process has not resulted in enough structural changes. This may be a legitimate concern, but within academic units it does appear that priorities have been set and decisions for reduction developed accordingly. But it also seems clear that Stanford can achieve its financial objectives without a fundamental redesign of the institution. This is happening in part because the institution doesn't absolutely have to make such a change. We can achieve the reduction without a major overhaul. More significant change may come if the financial situation worsens further or if a new administration, which will assume responsibility in the next fiscal year, can shape yet another effort.

The Process Question

Another reason why this process is not resulting in a more fundamental structural change is that its widely consultative, consensus-based nature does not lend itself to more targeted radical reductions. For example, it's virtually impossible to reach a consensus-based decision to close a school or to eliminate a major department. These kinds of actions must come from the top down. They must be accompanied by some consultation, to be sure, but strong leadership is the principal ingredient. It is simply very difficult to engage in such reforms with an administration that's in its final year and in a process that's as consultative as this one has been.

Managing Under Uncertainty

In the early to mid-'70s higher education went through a period of financial turmoil in which budgets were cut and some priorities were recast. One of the few bright spots of that difficult period, however, was the emergence of financial modeling as a tool for understanding and reshaping the institution. An important objective of the modeling work was the identification of financial equilibrium—a condition in which the growth of income and expense were roughly predictable and in parallel over the longer run (usually three to five years). Because of the strong growth of the '80s, financial equilibrium was more than exceeded. The question now is not whether we can continue to exceed an equilibrium condition, but whether we can even reach it. With the kinds of revenue constraints now in place, it seems that achieving equilibrium will continue to be a significant challenge. Continued reliance on productivity, reallocation, and occasional episodes of budget reduction will be the watchwords of the '90s.

Decentralization: A Hope But Not A Plan

As noted above, one of the objectives of this exercise has been to explore the potential of a more decentralized organizational structure. While considerable work needs to be done, there does seem to be potential for improving incentives and efficiencies in a system where responsibility and authority are more localized than in Stanford's current, relatively centralized system.

Reduction/Reengineering of Work

One of the unresolved challenges of this process—and the earlier Repositioning process—has been the reduction and redesign of work on the administrative side of the institution. The less difficult tasks of consolidation of units and the elimination of some kinds of services has been completed. What remains to do is far harder: actually to eliminate some of the work and to change the expectations of the processes in which that work is being done. No one in higher education, as best as I can tell, has done the kind of thing that Ford Motor Company did, for example, when it radically reengineered components of its administrative support structure, reducing headcount by as much as 75 percent while getting the same work done. It remains to be seen whether we have the creativity and the will to make such changes. At this point in history we certainly have the incentive.

Chapter 7

Market and Credit Perspectives

Ann L. Sowder

Senior Vice President,
Standard & Poor's Ratings Group

Higher education debt and creditworthiness are best viewed within the context of the overall credit markets. Let me begin by making some observations on the "bigger picture" within which higher education debt fits.

The credit markets of the 1980s have been characterized by many as "debt-crazed." In fact, the decade was dominated by overbuilding, overbuying, and overborrowing. As a result, there has been a severe deterioration of creditworthiness in this country. The median senior debt rating of industrial corporate borrowers is now "BB," a speculative grade category rating, compared to "A" ten years ago. During the '80s corporate downgrades exceeded upgrades by some 70 percent. Though the record was better in the municipal sector, downgrades still outpaced upgrades.

The '90s are seeing the "reequitization" of corporate America; debt is in disfavor; financial prudence and equity are "in." In the municipal sector pressures on ratings that were experienced throughout the 1980s came to a head in 1990 and 1991. These pressures include continued reduction of federal aid and shifts of service burdens to state and local governments; retrenchment of real estate values and construction after a period of explosive growth; drawdowns of budget reserves to their lowest levels in decades; and the arrival and now persistence of a recession.

In the higher education sector, credit quality in 1990 and 1991 has been

---

All ratings and outlooks included in this article were current as of November 6, 1991, and subsequently may have changed.

101

affected by the continuing decline in demand for higher education due to the decrease in the number of high school graduates. A reduction in freshman applicants to colleges and universities puts more pressure on management to control expenditure growth. At the same time, an increase in tuition to offset a lower matriculation rate could actually make the problems worse. Many public colleges and universities are also feeling the effects of their states' budget crunches as they fail to receive expected appropriations. With the onset and lingering of the recession, state schools have found themselves in an even tighter squeeze.

With this view of the larger environment, I'll turn now to how Standard & Poor's views higher education credit quality.

OVERVIEW OF RECENT RATING ACTIONS AND OUTLOOKS

Privates Colleges and Universities

Over the short-term, private higher education faces considerable challenges. First and foremost, demand pressures continue as a result of demographic shifts. However, this dynamic has been foreseen for many years. The effectiveness in past years of strategic planning is now becoming apparent.

Second, budget pressures continue to mount at many private institutions. Following five decades of post–World War II growth, budgets are strained by reduced demand and the difficulties of cutting costs in an era of no growth. This pressure is magnified at many major private universities because of the recent negative publicity surrounding indirect cost recoveries and the possible negative impact on the university research environment.

Despite these pressures, most private colleges and universities have entered this difficult era with significant flexibility. In fact, the rating distribution for private institutions has not substantially changed over the past year. S&P currently has nearly 150 unenhanced ratings outstanding on the general obligation debt of private colleges and universities. The greatest number of institutions (35) are still rated "A." The complete distribution is shown in Table A.

Rating changes during the past two years, detailed in Table B, have included slightly more downgrades than upgrades, but not markedly so. As an indicator of possible future rating changes, S&P assigns outlooks to ratings. "Positive" means a rating may be raised, and "negative" means a rating may be lowered, although neither indicator should be taken as an absolute precursor of a rating change. "Negative" rating outlooks currently outnumber

TABLE A
S&P Rated Private Colleges and Universities

AAA
California Institute of Technology, CA
Harvard University, MA
Massachusetts Institute of Technology, MA (c)
Princeton University, NJ
Princeton Theological Seminary, NJ (c)
Rockefeller University, NY
Stanford University, CA
Wellesley College, MA (c)
Yale University, CT

AA+
Amherst College, MA
Columbia University, NY
Dartmouth College, NHY
Massachusetts Institute of Technology, MA
Smith College, MA (c)
University of Richmond, VA (c)
Wellesley College, MA
Williams College, MA (c)

AA
Brown University, RI
Cornell University, NY
Duke University, NC
Hampton University, VA (c)
Middlebury College, VT
Oberlin College, OH
Pomona College, CA
Smith College, MA (c)
Swarthmore College, PA
University of Chicago, IL
University of Pennsylvania, PA
University of Southern California, CA
Vanderbilt University, TN
Wesleyan University, CT
Williams College, MA
Worcester Polytechnic Institute, MA (c)

AA-
Case Western Reserve University, OH
Colgate University, NY (c)
Davidson College, NC
Emory University, GA
Georgetown University, DC
Holy Cross College, MA (c)
Howard University, DC
Johns Hopkins University, MD
New York University, NY (c)

Northwestern University, IL
Radcliffe College, MA (c)
Smith College, MA
Teachers College-Columbia University, NY (c)
University of Richmond, VA
Vassar College, NY
Washington University, MO
Washington & Lee University, VA

A+
Boston College, MA
Boston University, MA
Carnegie Mellon University, PA
Colgate University, NY
Connecticut College, CT
Hampton University, VA
Hofstra University, NY (c)
Hollins College, VA (c)
Holy Cross College, MA
Kenyon College, OH
Loyola University of Chicago, IL
Mount Holyoke College, MA
New York University, NY
Reed College, OR
Rensselaer Polytechnic Institute, NY (c)
Rochester Institute of Technology, NY (c)
Tufts University, MA
Tulane University, LA
University of Rochester, NY
Worcester Polytechnic Institute, MA

A
Barnard College, NY
Bentley College, MA
Clark University, MA (c)
Clarkson College, NY (c)
Colby College, ME
Dickinson College, PA
Drew University, NJ (c)
Fairfield University, CT
Fordham University, NY
Gettysburg College, PA
Hofstra University, NY
Ithaca College, NY
Knox College, IL
Lafayette College, PA
Lehigh University, PA
Lesley College, MA
Macalester College, MN

(continued)

(Table A continued)

Medical College of Wisconsin, WI
Randolph Macon Women's College,
VARensselaer Polytechnic Institute, NY
Rhodes College, TN
Rochester Institute of Technology, NY
Stevens Institute of Technology, NJ (c)
Stonehill College, MA
St. Johns University, NY
St. Lawrence University, NY
St. Louis University, MO
St. Peter's College, NJ
Syracuse University, NY
Temple University, PA
Trinity College, CT
University of the Pacific, CA
University of the South, TN
Villanova University, PA
Wheaton College, MA

A-
Adelphi University, NY
Babson College, MA
Berklee College of Music, MA
Bryant College, RI
Clark University, MA
Depaul University, IL
Drexel University, PA
Elizabethtown College, PA
Hampden Sydney College, VA
Hartwick College, NY
Houghton College, NY
Iona College, NY
La Salle University, PA
Loyola University, LA
Pace University, NY
Providence College, RI
Rider College, NJ
Simmons College, MA
St. Michael's College, VT
Sweetbriar College, VA
University of Scranton, PA

BBB+
Abilene Christian University, TX
Florida Institute of Technology, FL
Lebanon Valley College, PA

Monmouth College, NJ
New England School of Law, MA
Russell Sage College, NY (c)
Siena College, NY
St. John's University, MN
University of Hartford, CT
University of San Diego, CA
Wilkes College, PA

BBB
Anderson University, IN
Ashland College, OH
Carroll College, WI
Dowling College, NY
Gannon College, PA
Gustavus Adolphus College, MN
Kings College, PA
Lycoming College, PA
Mercyhurst College, PA
New School for Social Research, NY
Nova University, FL
Philadelphia College of Textiles & Sciences, PA
Quinnipiac College, CT
San Francisco Conservatory of Music, CA
St. Bonaventure College, NY
Suffolk University, MA
Susquehanna University, PA
University of Denver, CO
University of New Haven, CT

BBB-
Incarnate Word College, TX
Manhattan College, NY
Moravian College, PA
Nichols College, MA
Seton Hill College, PA
St. Mary's College, MN
University of Evansville, IN
University of San Francisco, CA
Wagner College, NY
Western New England College, MA

BB
Fairleigh Dickinson University, NJ
University of Bridgeport, CT

(c) collateralized rating

Ratings reflect general obligation pledges; issues rated on a credit opinion, preliminary or private placement basis, as well as those backed by LOC's and bond insurance, are excluded.

"positive" outlooks by eight to three. Most outlooks, however, remain "stable," indicating that so far most institutions have managed heightened demand and budgetary pressures well.

TABLE B
Recent Rating Changes

	Former	Current
Berklee College of Music	BBB	A-
Boston College	A	A+
Fairleigh Dickinson University	A	BB
Johns Hopkins University	AA	AA-
Nichols College	BBB	BBB-
Rider College	BBB+	A-
St. Louis University	A-	A
Stevens Institute of Technology	A+	A(c)
Sweetbriar College	AA- (c)	A-
Wheaton College	A+	A-
University of Bridgeport	BBB+	BB

Public Colleges and Universities

Most public university ratings are affected by changes in a state's own rating of its general creditworthiness. The direction and degree of change will reflect institutional characteristics such as demand and financial position, as well as the institution's position in the state funding hierarchy.

The pattern of recent changes in the ratings of public colleges and universities is mixed, reflecting both upgrades and downgrades. (See Table C.) In early 1991 several public college and university ratings in Louisiana were raised as a result of an upgrade in the state's rating from BBB+ to A. In Vermont a corresponding change in the University of Vermont's rating was made in response to a downgrade in the state's rating from AA to AA-. Public college and university ratings do not always track in lockstep changes in the state's rating. As an example, while Kentucky's state rating remained at AA, the rating of Northern Kentucky University was changed from A to A- as a result, primarily, of its increasing debt burden.

S&P's currently negative rating outlook on several states has potential negative implications for public higher education ratings in those states. In particular, public higher education ratings in California, Michigan, and New York currently also have negative outlooks and may be hit by a downgrade at the state level.

TABLE C
Recent Rating Changes—Public Colleges and Universities

	Date	Direction of change	Former rating	Current rating	Outlook
FLORIDA				AA	Stable
Florida State Board of Regents	04-05-91	Up	A+	AA-	Stable
KENTUCKY					
Northern Kentucky University	03-11-91	Down	A	A-	Stable
LOUISIANA	12-19-90	Up	BBB+	A	Positive
Louisiana State University— Univ. of New Orleans	02-19-90	Up	BBB+	A	Positive
Louisiana State University— A&M College	02-19-91	Up	BBB+	A	Stable
Louisiana Technical University	02-20-91	Up	BBB	BBB+	Stable
McNeese State University	02-20-91	Up	BB+	BBB-	Stable
Nicholls State University	02-20-91	Up	BBB-	BBB	Stable
Northeast Louisiana University	02-13-91	Down	BBB	BBB-	Stable
Southeast Louisiana University	02-15-91	Up	BBB-	BBB	Stable
University of Southwestern Louisiana	02-15-91	Up	BBB	BBB+	Stable
NEW JERSEY	07-03-91	Down	AAA	AA+	Stable
Kean College	08-21-91	Up	BBB	A-	Stable
VERMONT	06-10-91	Down	AA	AA-	Stable
University of Vermont	06-11-91	Down	AA	AA-	Negative

Overall Sector Outlook

Judging by the small number of negative and positive outlooks relative to the total number of ratings outstanding, on an overall basis S&P assigns a "stable" outlook to higher education debt. In contrast to some of the observations and characterizations made recently, we do not see the higher education sector, or more specifically the ratings on higher education debt, as in a "crisis mode."

How do I reconcile this difference in perspective?

Clearly, higher education faces challenging times in the coming years. However, to agree that higher education faces declining growth, if not outright retrenchment, is a significantly different conclusion than to believe that higher education debt is in imminent danger of default. A rating is S&P's assessment of the likelihood of full and timely payment of debt service. As such, that assessment of default risk encompasses our overall view of the business and financial health of an institution. It also assumes, importantly, that payment of debt service on publicly issued and held debt is of preeminent importance to any institution that aims to continue as an ongoing concern. Accordingly, fulfilling one's debt service obligations is presumed to be such a priority that this budgetary item would be among the last to be sacrificed in a situation of insufficient resources.

We do not believe that higher education debt is in imminent danger of default or even suffering a significantly weakened ability to make payments as due. Ratings are assigned with a significant degree of resilience already factored in. Potential or likely financial pressures resulting from the down phase of a cycle are considered in assigning a rating in the first instance. Most of the financial pressures now facing higher education have been largely foreseen and are, we believe, adequately reflected in today's rating levels. Moreover, ratings have a dynamic element in that management is generally presumed to be intelligent and responsible enough to respond to financial pressures as they arise.

OVERVIEW OF RECENT FINANCING TRENDS

Three financing structures that are relatively new among higher education borrowers are:

Taxable Debt. There has been increased use of taxable debt, although not in significant amounts relative to total issuance. To lower the impact of its higher interest cost, taxable debt has mostly been used in a variable rate mode. S&P's fundamental credit analysis methods do not differ significantly for rating taxable debt.

Interest Rate Swaps. Because of their considerable financial resources, private higher education institutions are more likely than other types of municipal issuers to pursue innovative types of debt such as swaps. In addition to the structural features of these instruments, management's understanding of the mechanics and risks of these financing mechanisms is important. Each structure is analyzed on a case-by-case basis in relation to the institution's own financial flexibility.

Research Revenue-backed Financings. There has not been much recent activity in this area. A 1990 S&P publication discussed research revenue-backed financings by the University of Colorado and Utah State University.

More recently we have rated financings for purely research enterprises such as the Environmental Research Institute of Michigan, the Universities Space Research Association, and the National Center for Atmospheric Research. These ratings are significant as indicators of our comfort level with and willingness to rate strong research operations that are willing to structure their deals with strong legal protections.

INFLUENCE OF MANAGEMENT IN RATING PROCESS

Often we are asked whether management is a factor in determining a rating. The answer to that question is yes. However, management analysis is not so much a discrete rating factor as it is subsumed in other areas of analysis. At least three distinct aspects of management come into play:

1. demand management
2. financial (operational) management
3. debt management.

In assessing management ability, the following questions are considered:

Demand management. How well does management understand past application and enrollment trends? Does management have a plan for adapting to demographic changes? How will enrollment realignments fit within the institution's overall identity and mission? What resource needs are a consequence of adapting to a changed enrollment environment?

Financial management. How do budgeting practices reflect a more uncertain enrollment environment? Is there a conscious policy to underbudget in relation to enrollment? How stable is cash flow? How much flexibility is there to raise revenues or cut expenditures? To what extent do research activities add to or reduce financial flexibility? To what extent does endowment and gift income add to cash flow stability?

Debt management. How large is the capital improvement program and how dependent is it on future debt financing? Are deferred maintenance needs being addressed? Is there a history of private donations as an offset to debt financing?

There are no "standard" or "expected" responses to these questions. Judging the effectiveness of management depends in part on the quality of responses to these questions and, in part, on the demonstrated outcome of past management policies. Can "strong" management result in a higher rating? Probably not; that is, not higher than the fundamentals of demand strength and financial strength would suggest. It is our experience, however, that strong management under difficult circumstances can prevent or forestall a rating downgrade. An important implication of this observation is that debt ratings should not be equated to a "grading" of management. As a generalization, even the best management team cannot raise a rating higher than the level corresponding to the institution's fundamental demand and financial situation. Weak management can, however, cause an institution to achieve less than its highest "potential" rating.

CONCLUSION

Standard & Poor's, as a representative of the capital market's perspective on credit quality, believes that higher education management will appropriately and sufficiently respond to the challenges facing higher education so that overall credit quality will not change dramatically. We have not reached this conclusion on pure presumption but rather on the basis of examination.

The importance of your task and your apparent concern about it reinforce our confidence in your collective ability to see higher education safely through the coming decade's challenges.